"In *Permission to Grieve*, Toby Castle provides a practical resource for the church through the powerful communal practice of lament. This book is a helpful tool for ministry leaders as they facilitate ways for their congregations to actively respond to the suffering, injustices, and violence of our times."

—CINDY S. LEE, author of *Our Unforming: De-Westernizing Spiritual Formation*

"When I was a child growing up in Baltimore, Maryland, I found an incredible amount of solace in reading Lamentations. I never fully understood why until reading *Permission to Grieve*. The biblical chapter made me feel less alone in my personal suffering and the suffering I witnessed all around me. As Toby Castle brilliantly argues, this is by design. I can only hope that pastors and church leadership across the nation open their hearts to this truth and roadmap. As he makes abundantly clear, the future of the American church depends on it."

—DEWANDA WISE, filmmaker and activist

"*Permission to Grieve* is an act of radical love. In the same way that being a citizen of any nation requires active engagement, accountability, and thoughtful critique, so we have with the church. Here, Toby Castle dishes out his well-documented observations with a healthy serving of solution. He takes care to carve a path forward. What an absolutely generous and insightful read."

—ALANO MILLER, artist and screenwriter

"Forget the façade; grief and suffering are normal parts of the human experience. Being genuinely spiritual in the American Evangelical Christian tradition and being genuinely human are *not* mutually exclusive pursuits. To pull them apart is to pull apart what God has put together. Toby Castle exposes a flaw in American Evangelicalism, where notions of triumphalism and exceptionalism clash with Scripture and normalize a denialism that weakens both our faith and our witness."

—**BILL CODY**, retired evangelical pastor and community leader

"Humans suffer. People experience and witness difficult, exhausting, and painful events. These are part of the human condition. Evangelical churches and pastors too often numb the tragedies of life with cliches which, though well intentioned, ultimately do not ring true. Toby Castle invites us to encounter the events that break our hearts, to even embrace these events, recognizing that God meets us right at the center of our aches. Allow this book to give you the freedom to be venerable and to experience the presence of God in all of life."

—**KURT FREDRICKSON**, associate professor of pastoral ministry, Fuller Theological Seminary

Permission to Grieve

Permission to Grieve

*Lament as a Posture and Practice of Formation
in a Culture of Denial*

Toby D. Castle

Foreword by Soong-Chan Rah

WIPF *&* STOCK · Eugene, Oregon

PERMISSION TO GRIEVE
Lament as a Posture and Practice of Formation in a Culture of Denial

Wipf & Stock
An Imprint of Wipf and Stock Publishers
199 W. 8th Ave., Suite 3
Eugene, OR 97401

www.wipfandstock.com

PAPERBACK ISBN: 979-8-3852-2253-7
HARDCOVER ISBN: 979-8-3852-2254-4
EBOOK ISBN: 979-8-3852-2255-1

VERSION NUMBER 07/18/24

To those who have taught me to stand in the midst of ruins.
Kelley Castle, Andrew Burton, Paul Liddell,
Alano and DeWanda Miller, Bill Cody.

Contents

Foreword

IN MY ROLE AS a seminary professor, I have traveled to visit many churches and Christian ministries all over the world. My particular focus has been on studying U.S. churches that are experiencing significant demographic and cultural change. After many decades of visiting churches of all varieties and stripes, I still claim Christian faith as my spiritual identity and still believe in Jesus. But it has not been easy. Too many churches proclaimed and demonstrated a counterfeit gospel of American exceptionalism and dysfunctional triumphalism. Too many churches pursued the American dream for their congregation and their congregants, while ignoring the full gospel of Jesus Christ. Too many churches failed to engage the suffering of the cross and skipped to the triumph of the resurrection. Too many churches engaged in a false praise of a false god that gave them what they wanted rather than worshiping a God that suffered alongside them and called them to a profound lament. This book offers a snapshot of that dysfunctional narrative and imagination but also offers a biblical corrective.

I am honored that my student Toby Castle asked me to write the foreword for his work. And I am grateful for his profound effort and courage to write this book. The average seminary student can simply regurgitate what is taught in the classroom. They can still get a good grade in my class. The very good student takes the content of the class and the class curriculum and finds ways to thoughtfully analyze the teaching and apply the teaching in prophetic ways. In *Permission to Grieve*, Castle demonstrates that he is indeed a very good student and a very good teacher.

Foreword

Permission to Grieve does not offer simple answers. Instead, it plumbs the depths of Scripture, engaging even the ignored and neglected passages of lament that challenges the seductive power of the status quo. The North American Evangelical church has for too long sought to be the status quo and to maintain the status quo. We have sought ways to bathe in the luxuries of power, wealth, and position. We have become comfortable with lifting up examples of pastors and churches that choke on the riches of prosperity and power. We have been the mistress of Babylon rather than the shining light of Jerusalem. And we have praised and celebrated this dysfunction all along. This must end. And the end of this diseased imagination is not the triumphant downfall of the secular powers, but the quiet and necessary lament of the remnant, who still believe in the power of Christ's redemption.

Read this text. Allow this text to read you. Allow this text to read the church. And respond to the clarion call to lament as the church.

Soong-Chan Rah
Robert Munger Professor of Evangelism
Fuller Theological Seminary
Author of *The Next Evangelicalism* and *Prophetic Lament*

Acknowledgements

WITHOUT THE ROLE AND influence of certain people in my life, the writing and wrestling involved in this work would not have come to fruition. I am grateful first and foremost to the professors, mentors, and friends at Fuller Seminary who guided me through the adventure of academic inquiry, reflection, theological discovery, and practical imaginary. Many friends and family supported and cheered me on during my writing process. I owe a deep debt of gratitude to those who read my chapters and offered invaluable feedback.

Finally, this book would not be possible without the ever-present love and support of my wife, Kelley. Without her care, prayers, love, or encouragement this book would remain half-finished and a mere footnote in the lives, thoughts, and actions of our family, friends, and faith community.

Introduction

Grief and Suffering in a Culture of Denial

THE PASTOR, WITH A smiling face and well-meaning buoyancy at the end of the service, reminded the congregation as they began making their way to the exit that "we all have victory in Christ, if we believe we will take ground. God wills that we are more than conquerors, in every part of life. As you go about your week, be reminded, and take heart that, the truth is, the best is yet to come!"

It was a common refrain, exhortation, and benediction, framed as a mode of encouragement and reminder to all in the room that the God of the universe would never let them down and let no harm come to them if they placed their faith in God. I mean, life with Christ is meant to be enjoyed, not endured, right?

I heard this phrase often. Week-in and week-out. For a season, people around me would even hear me reflect my agreement with a hearty nod of the head, and supportive amen. Yet, after a while the perpetual reinforcement of and submission to uninterrupted success and victory with no mention of struggle, grief, or loss, the elements that help make us fully human, started wearing on me. It made me wonder if I was the only one who caught the incongruence between what was being said from the pulpit or the platform compared to the lived experience of some of those in the congregation—those who found a city like San Francisco a hard, difficult, violent, and often lonely city in which to live.

While lament is a difficult, complex, existential practice of faith-filled surrender, dissonance, anger, and sorrow, lament is also an appropriate and powerful response to pain, suffering, and grief. Soong-Chan Rah writes,

Introduction

"Lament . . . is a liturgical response to the reality of suffering and engages God in the context of pain and trouble."[1] Such pain and vulnerability are partly why many in evangelical communities seem to find the Psalms of lament or the book of Lamentations difficult texts to relate to. Some followers of Christ do not allow themselves to be exposed to or have examples of painful, visible, and courageous vulnerability. As such, those in North American Evangelical faith communities live with an element of a passive narrative to pain and suffering that eventually equates to a thin veil of ignorant denial.

Kathleen O'Connor, in *Lamentations and the Tears of the World*, writes, "For readers who live with denial, as the United States capitalist society requires, Lamentations makes difficult reading."[2] Covert despair or repressed hopelessness, as Douglas J. Hall explains, characterizes the atmosphere of North American and Western society.[3] Unlike those who live on the margins of society—often described biblically as the poor, the widow, or the orphan—trauma and violence for many is hidden or denied as a coping mechanism used to deal with the complexities of life. This is a survival tactic used by many, for we "humans know at a deeper level . . . that survival depends upon hope."[4]

Consequentially, the North American evangelical church,[5] as a way to combat this existential reality, has seemingly substituted faith as certainty; doubt as unbelief; and anger with God as dishonorable and disrespectful. Even from the pulpit and platform, preachers and teachers often misplace lament as disrespectful and an ignominious practice that no longer has a place in a community's or individual's mode of worship. By removing the

1. Rah, *Prophetic Lament*, 21.

2. O'Connor, *Lamentations and the Tears*, 4.

3. Hall, "Despair in Pervasive Ailment," 91.

4. King, *Letter from Birmingham Jail*, 189.

5. Public Theologian D. J. Smit in his essays regarding the church highlights six specific expressions that make the church unique to other organizations or institutions globally. Throughout this book I will be leaning in to his terminology, while focusing on the evangelical community and, where required, delineating this with the church in San Francisco, California. Smit describes these six expressions as (i) Ecumenical (either local, regional, or international); (ii) consisting of a denomination; (iii) a community of faith or believers in the form of a congregation; (iv) the posture and practice as a God-worshiping community; (v) a group of individual believers in community (as expressed in one's personal, private, and public lives); and (vi) the church as believers (individuals and groups) participating in social initiatives and actions, together with others. Smit, *Essays in Public Theology*.

Introduction

practice of lament as a central tool of worship in the formation of God's people, the North American evangelical church engages in a willful, but unintended, posture of *forgetfulness*, what I describe as a *willful non-re-membering* and a *posture and practice of denial.* This becomes, therefore, an expression of injustice for the privileged-passivity and forgetfulness of a privilege that perpetuates injustice.

When we read Scripture, lament and the expression of grief are common experiences. The Psalms, Jeremiah, and Lamentations—to name a few—give language and voice to grief, suffering, and loss. Lament is not counter to the Judeo-Christian way of life but needs to be remembered, reimagined, recognized, and embraced as a faithful, courageous part of the way of Jesus through the Christlike disciplines of prayer, worship, justice, witness, hope, and formation.

Turning contextually to San Francisco as a case study, how do followers of Jesus, in what many describe as one of the least Christian cities in North America,[6] engage with the difficulties of everyday life if they are taught, reminded, encouraged, or equipped with an ecclesial worldview that being in Christ means we always win? Why does North American evangelical theology maximize a culture of fame, profit, triumphalism, and success, while all too often failing to engage in the creative suffering of God that is so pertinent throughout Scripture in the form of public and private lament? Could it be found in a thin understanding and expression of the gospel? Has the evangelical American church shifted away from a thicker expression of Jesus[7] in public spaces and places? Has the North American

6. James, *Church Planting.*

7. In 2012, just prior to his passing, my mentor and friend, Glen H. Stassen, wrote what many believed to be his seminal work, *A Thicker Jesus: Incarnational Discipleship in a Secular Age.* In it Stassen writes, "In *A Thicker Jesus,* I am asking two questions: (1) how to find a faithful and solid identity for faith and ethics; and (2) how that identity can be a compass in our rapidly changing and interactive age" (loc. 179). Speaking about leading theological writers and thinkers of the twentieth century, such as Bonhoeffer, Martin Luther King, Clarence Jordan, André Trocmé, Muriel Lester, and others, Stassen continues, "They all wrote with a thick, historically-embodied, realistic understanding of Jesus Christ as revealing God's character and thus providing norms for guiding our lives. They did not reduce Jesus to a thin principle or high ideal or only doctrinal affirmation without solid grounding in his actual history. They all wrote with a holistic understanding of the Lordship of Christ or sovereignty of God throughout all of life and all of creation. They opposed a two-kingdoms or body-soul or temporal-eternal dualism that blocks God's guidance in Christ from applying to a secular realm. They all wrote with a strong call for repentance from captivity to ideologies such as nationalism, racism, and greed. And their actions, their actual practices, fit their written theological ethics"

church been distracted by its mission and so bifurcated its presence in the community from its pursuit of power, wealth, and political influence over and above the complexity of suffering, doubt, liminality, and grief? Has the cultural pursuit of American exceptionalism muted presence of sorrow, heartache, pain, and loss in the public and private expression of church? These are some of the questions I seek to address throughout this book.

A Growing Wedge

As I continued to explore the nature of grief and loss in the evangelical community in North America, lament was not and has not been a pervasive feature of San Francisco's Christian expression, let alone its teaching or theology. In most cases, the voice of lament appeared to be muffled, muted, or eclipsed altogether in favor of a resurrection hope and an emphasis of fortitude in circumstances of suffering. Such battles were reframed as moments of and for character and/or spiritual formation. People would be laid-off from their jobs, be unable to find a husband or wife, be racially vilified, lose family to cancer, or see friends pass away from COVID-19.

It was in these seasons of sorrow and distress that require the practice lament as an appropriate and God-hopeful response. Yet, the reaction to such moments of despair, loss, or grief is often a concoction of empty platitudes or rosy reassurances that fail to give voice or recognition to the reality of the individual's or community's situation. Dan Allender writes, "Christians often assume our conflict with God was finished when we converted. . . . But the battle is not over with conversion—though it is the decisive victory that assures the outcome of the war, it is hardly the last and final fight."[8] It was becoming clear that the local faith community, in San Francisco—and across North America, had misunderstood the value and impact of lament as part of individual and corporate Christian formation. For a city like San Francisco, I began to wonder if the absence of the

---

(loc. 444). Throughout this book, when speaking of a thicker Jesus, within the purview of lament, I will be referring to and leaning on Stassen's perspective. As teachers and leaders in the evangelical, North American church begin to witness to a "thicker Jesus" in their everyday practices of worship, I believe which lament will no longer be forgotten or misunderstood or misappropriated, but be remembered and reestablished as a Christian discipline and practice imperative to the formation and reimagination of the body of Christ in public and private spaces and places.

8. Allender, "Hidden Hope in Lament," para. 8.

theology and practice of lament in public and private settings contributed to the growing wedge between the church and the city.

San Francisco: A City like No Other

San Francisco comprises thirty-six neighborhoods and, pre-pandemic, had a population just shy of 875,000 people.[9] The pandemic caused a population decrease, where multi-billion-dollar tech companies moved interstate, and the impact of homelessness on the city became increasingly visible.[10] In late March 2022, the *San Francisco Standard* reported, "Between April 2020 and July 2021, the city's population declined by 58,764 residents, according to new figures from the U.S. Census Bureau. San Francisco's drop represents a 6.7% drop in population and places the city second only to New York County (better known as Manhattan) as the county with the greatest drop nationwide."[11] Such a shift in the population was emblematic of some of the changes experienced in the city throughout the pandemic. As the pandemic continued, it became increasingly obvious that the local church did not have the language, tools, theology, or practices to help the people and its community express their experiences effectively. The absence of lament was one of these tools.

Christopher B. James in *Church Planting in Post-Christian Soil* writes, "Worship and mission are complementary centripetal and centrifugal forces . . . which envisions mission as both evangelism and service."[12] He continues, "Envisioning church as a contrast community of disciples . . . has a special utility in an environment in which the general culture gives little support to Christian values."[13] While many churches maintained a cadence in the lead-up to the pandemic, it was becoming evident that such praxis was lacking the deeper elements found in discipleship and deeply formed and vulnerable practices, like lament, that many people were craving.

Akin to conversion, there can be no lament without surrender. "To lament," writes Allender, "is to cry out to God with our doubts, our incriminations of him and others, to bring a complaint against him—is the context for surrender." Allender continues, "Surrender—the turning of our heart

---

9. Thompson, "Yep. SF's Population Decline."

10. Thompson, "Yep. SF's Population Decline."

11. Thompson, "Yep. SF's Population Decline," para. 4.

12. James, *Church Planting*, 76.

13. James, *Church Planting*, 76.

over to him, asking for mercy, and receiving his terms for restoration—is impossible without battle. To put it simply, it is inconceivable to surrender to God unless there is a prior, declared war against him."[14]

To declare war against God is not a common phrase one would hear in an evangelical setting. Whether it be too aggressive or be perceived to be a practice that fails to bring honor or reverent fear to God, to lament is to wage a warlike, violent allegation of abandonment to God. To echo Emmanuel Katongole, to lament "in the midst of suffering . . . takes the form of arguing and wrestling with God,"[15] and so "becomes a way of naming what is going on, of standing and of hoping in the midst of ruins."[16]

This work of this book is designed to equip ministry and church leaders to reimagine the posture, practice, ecclesiology, and theology of lament in the local church. Articulated intentionally as a theopraxis of lament, this enterprise is compelled by the vision that the local church is called to be just peacemakers (or shalom makers) and bridge-builders in their everyday engagement with the people and the city they are called to love and serve. In moments of despair, heartache, loss, or anguish the local church is called to seek God's wisdom, sit with, and contend for others in times of liminal uncertainty, and help provide space and language for and permission to grieve. To lament, in such moments, is to help people trust God when everything seems lost.

In the first part of this book, I introduce the theology and practice of lament in the context of the wider evangelical church in North America. Once situated in this cultural frame, within the North American evangelical milieu of triumphalism and success, this book explores the posture and practice of victory and overcoming up and against the current culture and climate of San Francisco, CA. Lastly, I explore the conflicting currents of Christian faith and expression within the city of San Francisco and so frame the relative cultural and theological inversions that currently make these two realities missionally contrary to one another.

Secondly, I review works related to the posture, practice, and theological formation of lament for the church. In the first section I address the role that lament plays in the lives of those who say they follow Jesus. In section 2 I exegete Lamentations using the works of O'Connor, F. W. Dobbs-Allsopp, Nancy C. Lee, and Carleen Mandolfo to focus and frame the origins, flow,

---

14. Allender, "Hidden Hope in Lament," para. 7.

15. Katongole. *Born from Lament*, xvi.

16. Katongole. *Born from Lament*, 48

and function of lament in the lives of everyday followers of Jesus. Finally, I examine in section three various sources pertaining to the praxis of lament that serves as theological and practical patterns for public witness in missional contexts of injustice and biblical peacemaking.

As you continue to read, you'll dive into and develop a theological foundation for the posture, practice, and position of lament in the role of discipleship and peacemaking for evangelicals in North America. Firstly, I position lament as the central, missing practice in Christian formation in evangelical faith communities. Secondly, I recognize lament as a protest against the world as it is and the brokenness that is inevitable with the human condition. Lastly, I situate lament next to American evangelicalism and highlight its theological incompatibilities, witnessing to the imperative, yet absence, of lament in evangelical formation. I then frame some practical goals around a pilot discipleship group within the context of lament, the city of San Francisco, and Christian community. Through research questions, we'll explore with participants in this pilot discipleship group how lament is perceived as a practice of formation, witness, and communal justice. The goal of this pilot discipleship group is to frame lament as an incarnational impulse out into the city that calls for the participation of those who follow Jesus. The design and strategy of this pilot discipleship group is framed around a holistic formation model.

Lastly, I provide a detailed outline of the strategy and assessment of this pilot discipleship group program designed to form faith communities through the practice of lament. I assess this pilot discipleship group program using a combination of qualitative and quantitative modes of assessment that include discussion groups, survey questions, Likert scale questionnaires, and interviews that asked participants to be reflexive in their experience and formation.

Post-pandemic, one becomes curious if the North American evangelical community has created space for and given time to deep reflection specific to its thin, truncated response to social and physical isolation. The practice and presence of lament helps communities of Jesus respond more effectively and appropriately with those they are proximal to in their city. It is imperative that those who say they follow Jesus use their social imaginary, associated with lament, to help faith-based communities bridge the growing gap between the local church and its local community in cities like San Francisco. This is the hope and pursuit of this book.

1

Lament

Wisdom Language of Grief and Suffering

"What is most needed is what is most unacceptable—
an articulation that redefines the situation and that
makes way for new gifts about to be given"

—Walter Brueggemann

A mentor of mine, a cisgender woman of color, affirmed to me over and over again, "It's not the context we find ourselves in, but our response to it that's most important." How the local church leads and serves its people in their response to suffering is central to this paper. Lament, I contend, is the language of Christian grief and suffering. Lament is a theological and ecclesial posture and practice, a "battle cry against God that paradoxically voices a heart of desire and ironic faith in his goodness."[1] To lament is to expose oneself bravely to the reality of one's experience, originally oriented towards God as the one who would fulfil, protect, provide, and defend. Yet, when one is exposed to death, destruction, or disappointment, lament becomes a way of declaring injustice and disillusionment, either personal or communal, to God who can handle our displeasure, as a concrete spiritual and liturgical step towards hope.

1. Allender, "Hidden Hope in Lament," para. 9.

1

William Blaine-Wallace writes, "When grieving and aggrieved persons bring their sorrow, suffering, and trauma into intentionally constructed and serendipitously discovered community, lamentational relation is established."[2] Lament cultivates common ground and relational intimacy, and helps create a *common memory* that, in community, allows people to walk with and carry one another's grief as they move towards a collective hope.

The evangelical church in North America, like the greater cultural milieu it springs from, is hyper-individualized, hyper-masculine, and hyper-victorious.[3] As the church moves away from its hyper-individualized, hyper-success-focused orientation and opens itself to the blessing of communal grief and suffering, it will slowly but surely move towards practices of shalom and bridge-building that is fundamental to the mission of God. There is an indivisible relationship in the Bible between peace (shalom) and justice. Indeed, it must be remembered that justice is a fundamental dimension of shalom.

These movements are essential in cultivating deep, embodied hope central to the gospel. Such recognition of grief and suffering will not lead people to a reduced superficial, false, thin hope, one that can be substituted by the pursuit of affluence, control, and political power. Instead, followers of Jesus will be exposed to an expansive, collective hope that speaks truth to power while highlighting the realities of alienation, marginalization, spiritual hunger, and meaninglessness that is often synonymous to the triumphalism that is so closely linked to the current North American evangelical community.[4]

Found in the Old Testament and New Testament, lament can be framed uniquely as poetry and wisdom language. Although primarily contained in a collection of works known as wisdom literature (*Kethuvim*) in books such as Job, Psalms, Ecclesiastes, Proverbs, and Song of Songs, this collection of

2. Blaine-Wallace, *When Tears Sing*, 6.

3. O'Connor, *Lamentations and Tears*, 52.

4. O'Connor, in *Lamentations and Tears of the World*, refers often to Canadian theologian Douglas John Hall's critique and social analysis of North American culture of the twentieth century, where he proposes that people in the West have lived under a growing, deadening blanket of covert despair. Described by O'Connor, this covert despair is often "fostered by wealth, power, and violence" (xiv) that distracts the general population from engaging with their own moments of personal and collective trauma. This cultural thread of covert despair will be analyzed throughout this paper over and against the North American church's pursuit of power and influence and subsequent victorious Christianity that has arguably left the faith community unable and ill-equipped theologically to deal with and speak to the complexities of public violence and trauma such as white supremacy and racism in North American society.

literature also includes several more books including Lamentations, Esther, Daniel, Ezra, Nehemiah, and First and Second Chronicles. The wisdom writings "appear to have come together during a time of transition in Israel. The shift was not so much political or even religious as it was existential."[5] As Israel, God's chosen people, began questioning their prosperity, health, righteousness, and effective *chosen-ness* during this transitionary, liminal period they were discovering that even though they were following Torah, remaining obedient, and—in the context of Job—thought they had been righteous, they still became sick and suffered grief, devastation, and loss. Michael Card writes,

> Israel sometimes felt the tension on a national level as well, most notably in the time of Jeremiah, when Babylonian "sinners" conquered God's people, the Jews. These questions, which confronted the centuries-old wisdom embodied in Torah Obedience, eventually found a voice in Wisdom Writings. From this we see that the collection is not as much about wisdom as it is the perceived inadequacy of wisdom.[6]

Lament was and still is a tool for the people of God to seek God's wisdom in moments of grief, despair, and suffering. With examples found prominently in Job and Lamentations, we witness the people of God questioning, accusing, and blaming God when they are found to be at the lowest. The process of lament, at its most basic level, is God preparing God's people, albeit passively, for a deeper understanding and thicker trust of God and God's presence (*hesed*). The practice of lament, therefore, needs to be remembered and reengaged "as a resource for the work of reclaiming our humanity, for breaking through our denial, personal and social, and for teaching us compassion"[7] in all areas of our walk with Jesus, our neighbor, our context, and ourselves. To lament is to pursue shalom.

Lament and Liminality—The Creation of Sacred Space

The posture and practice of lament ascends characteristically from contexts and moments of oppression, violence, marginality, and ostracism. Consistently throughout the Old Testament, lament has been a response to exile, sickness, death, and the conquest and destruction of the city of Jerusalem

5. Card, *Sacred Sorrow*, 41.

6. Card, *Sacred Sorrow*, 42.

7. Card, *Sacred Sorrow*, xiv

(specifically in Lamentations and Jeremiah). In the New Testament, lament is less prevalent, but still present. The death of Lazarus (John 11), Jesus' lamenting over Jerusalem (Luke 13:34), Jesus praying in the Garden of Gethsemane (Matt 26:36–46; Luke 22:39–46), and the death of Jesus (Matt 27:45–56; Mark 15:21–41; Luke 23:44–49) are some of the more explicit moments of lament in the New Testament.

These moments of lament create periods of liminality where people are provided spaces of uncertainty to process, grieve, and wrestle. Sang Hyun Lee, in *From a Liminal Place: An Asian American Theology*, defines liminality and liminal space as

> a space where a person is freed up from their usual ways of think-ing and acting and is therefore open to radically new ideas. Freed from structure, persons in liminality are also available to genu-ine communion (communitas) with others. Liminal space is also where a person can become acutely aware of the problems of the existing structure. A person in a liminal space, therefore, often re-enters social structure with alternative ideas of human relatedness and also with a desire to reform the existing social structure.[8]

Lament is a liminal practice. "The word [liminal] originally described a threshold, the space in a doorway that is neither in nor out. Liminal times can be scary and downright dangerous because we hover between systems. We leave behind old norms and roles and haven't yet entered new ones."[9] This transitionary space could be one reason why, in difficult times, some people fail to gravitate towards lament. If a person or community is expe-riencing a disruption of grief, like a death in the family, to add a layer of insecurity seems counterintuitive. "Liminality [like lament] kicks us out of old routines, which not only gives us those apocalyptic epiphany moments but also sets us up to do something about what's revealed to us."[10] Such change and transition are what many experienced during the pandemic.

But now that the pandemic is in the rearview mirror, many faith lead-ers seem to perceive this *new normal* as an excuse to return to what they know. This posture and practice functions more as a retreat and return to what is known, what one sees as certain—masked as a soothing balm from their weekly Sunday cadence—instead of leaning into what the Spirit of God may have planned for God's people, the church.

8. Lee, *From a Liminal Place*, 6.

9. Ward, *When the Universe Cracks*, 17.

10. Ward, *When the Universe Cracks*, 17.

Walter Brueggemann writes, "What is most needed [in the liminal space of lament] is what is most unacceptable—an articulation that redefines the situation and that makes way for new gifts about to be given. Without a public arena for the articulation of gifts that fall outside our conventional rationality, we are fated for despair."[11] Lament experienced liminally becomes a new, positive spiritual expression and creative practice of social change—personally and collectively or individually and corporately—where the Spirit engages one's social imagination for the redemptive transformation of their community. Such an understanding of lament helps people reimagine the transformative power of this practice. Liminality, when participating with the Spirit, forms new gifts and new insights and new revelation for those who create space for the Spirit to move in their lives.

Humans cannot, however, exist in a liminal space for an extended period of time. Although Christians live continually in an eschatological tension of the now, but not yet, humanity seeks the certainty and clarity of resolution. This is what makes the *liminal space of lament* so unique, powerful, and transformative. Lament is not an end in and of itself. Lament only lasts from a finite time, then asks the individual to re-engage with society. Lee writes,

> Human beings cannot exist in liminality for an indefinite period of time. They have to enter some structure, at least for survival as human beings. Thus, social change involves a dialectic movement between liminality/communitas and structure. Without occasional immersion into liminality/communitas, society becomes static.[12]

It is imperative, therefore, that faith leaders, pastors, and the people of God return to and engage with a renewed understanding of lament. Its practice and understanding will create intentional space for liminal transformation and the creation of a new social imaginary for the people of God, on mission with God, for the redemption of the world. Ultimately, the liminal liturgy of lament functions in multiple ways. To lament is not to grumble or complain or moan as the ultimate purpose of its practice. To lament means to properly engage with grief with a God we deeply trust, despite the circumstance in which we find ourselves. "Lament leads to petition which leads to praise for God's response to the petition."[13] Lament brings God's reality and perspective in liminal and transitional moments so the people of God can then journey together in community. This is the beauty of liminality and lament.

11. Brueggemann, *Prophetic Imagination*, 63.

12. Lee, *From a Liminal Place*, 6.

13. Rah, *Prophetic Lament*, 21.

2

Evangelical Victory, Triumphalism, Success

Truth-telling is an act of survival because it affirms the
humanity of victims, gives them agency, and places a wedge
between their experience of suffering and its expression.

—Dr. Kathleen O'Connor

TRIUMPHAL, PERPETUAL SUCCESS ORIENTED Christian exceptionalism is
a cancer on the church. Not to oversimplify nor to become reductionist
in this critique, the overwhelming mantra that flows from the platforms
and pulpits of North American evangelical churches separates the American church from the experiences of the people the church is attempting
to serve. It is a fundamental class of narratives. Rah writes, "A triumphant
and success-oriented narrative limits the twenty-first-century American
evangelical theological imagination. The narrative of triumph silences a
narrative of suffering."[1]

One nuance here is not that Jesus' death and resurrection has failed to
conquer death (1 Cor 15:55–57) or inhibited God's people from receiving
eternal life—giving us victory through our Lord Jesus Christ. Another nuance is that the North American evangelical church desires the victory and

1. Rah, *Prophetic Lament*, 72.

6

celebration of Jesus (Easter Sunday) without experiencing his death on the cross (Good Friday) or the liminal, dark night of the soul (Holy Saturday).

Lament, in moments of despair, grief, sorrow, pain, death, or oppression provides the people of God with the space and agency to imagine, protest, trust, and dare God to help them navigate the complexity and agony of grief and loss. Lament offers a way of bearing witness and giving language to pain and sorrow in the form of poetic truth-telling that helps those who continue to put their trust in God as an act of survival, agency, and hope.[2]

Specific to this vision is an intentional move away from the triumphalism and success-driven exceptionalism that is synonymous with North American evangelicalism.[3] Arising from a deep theological deficiency that seeks the resurrection of Jesus without his death on the cross, this book seeks to guide those who are willing towards a new narrative that cultivates a creative, missional engagement that helps give voice and so equip people who, in the midst of suffering, can find voice, become poetic truth-tellers. The hope is that followers of Jesus will then seek to find a place where *deferred hope* takes the form of lament, where people in San Francisco can stand in the midst of ruins. Lament is what sustains and carries Christian agency in the midst of suffering. To be courageous[4] is to exhibit the practice

2. Dr. Kathleen O'Connor, in *Lamentations and Tears of the World*, describes a poetry of truth-telling in the following way. "Truth-telling is an act of survival because it affirms the humanity of victims, gives them agency, and places a wedge between their experience of suffering and its expression. Lamentations is ancient poetry of truth-telling, an act of survival that testifies to the human requirement to speak the unspeakable, to find speech in traumatized numbness, and, to . . . assert boldly the sheer fact of pain" (5–6).

3. Soong-Chan Rah writes, in *Prophetic Lament: A Call for Justice in Troubled Times*, "A triumphant and success-oriented narrative limits the twenty-first century American evangelical theological imagination. The narrative of triumph silences a narrative of suffering." (72) It is this lack of imagination and theological complexity that has led the North American evangelical church believe, inappropriately, that it holds a unique position in American society. While this is not a specific focus of this paper, it must be noted that its lack of social and prophetic imagination, to hold in-tension that of death and life, joy, and pain, or hope and despair has created a false belief that the North American evangelical church is unique and privileged over and above their neighbors. Rah continues, "The dismantling of privilege requires the disavowal of any pretense of exceptionalism" (72). So, as a community we are encouraged to acknowledging our shortcomings, explore steps towards vulnerability, seek to demystify the myth of perfectionism, and share one-another's grief. In doing so, in the form of lament, we as the church begin to step away from various perceptions of false pretense and so embody a community that seeks to be like Jesus in the practice of just peacemaking and bridge-building in a city like San Francisco that on a daily basis encounters the realities of grief and sorrow in the lives of others.

4. Brené Brown, in *Daring Greatly: How the Courage to be Vulnerable Transforms the Way We Live, Love, Parent, and Lead,* speaks intentionally to the virtue and practice of

of lament as an intentional work of hope in its theological, cultural, and practical dimensions. To lament is to embody trust in God when one feels God has failed them. It is a discipline that the local church in San Francisco desperately needs. Without lament, it is feared that the church in San Francisco will continue to become more marginalized and isolated.

Chaos and Peace

San Francisco is a difficult city. Unlike other parts of the United States, the cultural pressures, presence of tech, the reality of homelessness, the cost of living, and the absence of community makes the cultivation of community, especially Christian community, challenging. If people are not working long hours or trying to make rent or attempting to find rest in the city, then they are escaping the chaos to find relief and peace outside the city, at every possible moment.

The theological, cultural, and practical dimensions of lament are fundamental to peacemaking and bridge-building in a city that is becoming more and more known for its chaos[5] than its peace. By sowing seeds in a cohort-like community of local church leaders, it is hoped they will then build communities of belonging in their own way that replicate and demonstrate the power and gift of vulnerability as they share and grieve together in public and private spaces, as an intentional practice of hope.

Then, as the people of God return and remember their grief and begin to explore the richness of sharing their pain and frustration with God, they will find a depth of comfort and care that is strangely familiar. By not passing over their suffering, but engaging with it directly, the people of God will find, in this courageous engagement, a posture and practice of lament that will help all the people of God, on mission with God, create new narratives of hope, courage, and belonging. As such, we all have the opportunity to commune with God in the full spectrum of our common, everyday life—the good, the bad, and the ugly. Such encounters equip people to be brave truth-tellers, to speak to the pain and sorrow of the city, and to hear the voice of those who suffer with us. Lament honors voices of pain while edging people ever closer to a narrative of hope, surrender, and restoration.

---

courage in moments of despair, pain, and sorrow. Her work will be touched on through this paper. It is hoped that the overlap between her work and the various dimensions of lament will become more explicit to the reader.

5. Hagstrom, "CEO Blasts San Francisco."

3

San Francisco
A Missional Approach

⁸ Record my misery; list my tears on your
scroll are they not in your record?

⁹ Then my enemies will turn back when I call for
help. By this I will know that God is for me.

—Psalm 56:8-9 (NIV)

San Francisco is not like most American cities. Holding tight to its perception as America's most progressive and liberal city, San Francisco has the smallest churchgoing population in the United States. In 2017, 61 percent of the population did not attend church and one-third of all residents claim no religious affiliation.[1] To a broader extent, the Bay Area—which includes San Francisco, Daly City, Oakland, Berkley, and Walnut Creek (to the east); Santa Clara, San Jose, and Sunnyvale (to the south); and Napa, Santa Rosa, Mill Valley, and Sonoma (to the north)—in 2017 was described as the most dechurched[2] region in the United States. If San Francisco and the Bay Area

1. "Church Attendance Trends."
2. For this point and throughout this book, where necessary, the term nonchurched signifies a person within a given community who is not connected to a Christian faith community. In some cases, people who identify as nonchurched are now classified as

9

maintain similar trajectories with the rest of the United States, churches in the city would have experienced a significant downturn in church attendance, engagement, and participation,[3] despite the presence of and growth around online services as a creative response to the pandemic.

In a city where the existence of the church and the praxis of public Christianity is the least present in the country, church leaders and Christian faith communities in San Francisco are at a reckoning point. San Francisco is not like any other city. Its polycentric mosaic of neighborhoods makes it one of the most diverse cities in the country. In this context, the church has a unique, missional opportunity that calls for a different form of creative praxis compared to other cities in the United States.

Frank Newport, in a Gallup news article, wrote, "One of the traditional roles of religious individuals and religious entities has been to serve a positive, integrative, pro-social, charitable function in crisis situations. When it comes to confronting contemporary social turmoil, communities of faith have always played an important role in working toward solutions."[4] It seems, however, the creative praxis of church for many evangelical communities in the presence of complex social grief and trauma has been reduced to a service-centric, myopic, disembodied presence in a city that fails to resonate with the polymodal needs and narratives of San Francisco. Al Tizon, in *Whole and Reconciled*, writes,

> In our increasingly globalizing, diversifying, fracturing world, the church needs to recover the full message of Jesus Christ, the embodiment of the kingdom. Since the time of the apostles and until Christ returns, the God of mission has sent the church to proclaim, demonstrate, and live out this gospel throughout the whole world.[5]

Tizon's full message is a creative, missional call for faith leaders and churches in San Francisco to exegete the city, listen to the Spirit, move intentionally, reflect on the lessons of the COVID pandemic, and engage with their social imaginary in new, creative, and missional ways. This is the role that lament can play in public and private spaces.

---

dechurched. This nomenclature means they were, at one point, connected to a Christian faith community but no longer identify as such.

3. Kinnaman, "Year Out."

4. Newport, "Religion and the COVID-19 Virus," para. 20.

5. Tizon, *Whole and Reconciled*, 82.

Emerging from the pandemic and simply returning to a highly produced, ninety-minute service, is an example of an incomplete, thin, reductionist understanding of the calling of faith communities on mission with God. The data suggests that this approach has failed to resonate with the people of San Francisco and its thirty-six neighborhoods.

The people of God are continuously and repeatedly called to hear, remember, and so embody its missional calling, not by creating space between what may be perceived as sacred or secular, holy or profane, in or out, but by leaning in, making visible, and demonstrating the reign of the kingdom of God by hearing who God is calling people on mission to become. Fitch affirms this position when he writes, in *Faithful Presence*,

> The difference between the church and the world is therefore not spatial, that is, between where God is and where God is not. There is no *in here* and *out there* when it comes to the church. Instead, the church in essence experiences God's presence visibly now, ahead of time when God shall visibly reign among the whole world. The difference between the church and the world then is just a matter of timing. The church experiences the kingdom ahead of time. The rest of world is heading there; they just don't know it yet.[6]

San Francisco has always been a city ready to receive the gospel of the kingdom of God. The local church is being asked to remember and return to the practices of God's people that bought compassion, courage, and intimacy. In slowing down and remembering, the local church will be given the opportunity to hear what God is doing, hear and feel the rhythms of the city, recognize the need of and for embodied presence, and cultivate a creative, missional praxis that is contextualized to the need and mosaic of San Francisco. This cultural exegesis is imperative to the life of the church in city.

Michael J. Gorman, in *Becoming the Gospel: Paul, Participating, and Mission*, frames missional interpretation, exegesis, engagement, and praxis within the context of and participating in the mission of God. He defines with clarity the term missional, its use and application when he writes,

> A missional hermeneutic is grounded in the theological principle of the *missio Dei*, or mission of God. This term summarizes the conviction that the Scriptures of both Testaments bear witness to a God who, as creator and redeemer of the world, is already on a mission. Indeed, God is by nature a missional God, who is seeking not just to save "souls" to take to heaven someday, but to restore

---

6. Fitch, *Faithful Presence*, 39.

and save the created order: individuals, communities, nations, the environment, the world, the cosmos. This God calls the people of God assembled in the name of Christ—who was the incarnation of the divine mission—to participate in this *missio Dei*, to discern what God is up to in the world, and to join in.[7]

It is this participatory, tripartite approach—a faith community's ecclesial philosophy, posture, and practice—of the *missio Dei* that is imperative to the church's prophetic imagination and missional engagement. When engaged innovatively and courageously, faith communities cultivate divergent, unorthodox practices that become more expansive, polycentric, and contextual to the cities they find themselves in.

Expanding a faith community's missional philosophy, posture, and practice is not easy. Sandra Maria Van Opstal, in *The Next Worship*, affirms "congregations typically do not adapt their worship to represent minority communities."[8] Missional creativity is a rigorous, theological and ecclesial wrestle. One that is led by the Holy Spirit towards an expansive, cocreative engagement with, in, and through a community of cultivating relationships that permeate the city. In a city like San Francisco, with many diverse expressions, neighborhoods, and social concerns that repeatedly make national and international headlines,[9] the call and demand of the local church to truly be missional and so walk with God in Christ has never been higher.

Missional creativity is also centered on biblical justice as its social, everyday expression. Tim Keller, in *Generous Justice*, writes, "Biblical justice is 'social', because it is about relationships."[10] Missional creativity engages contextually the culture and ecosystem of the people they are called to serve.

Thinking practically and contextually, concrete examples of missional creativity, associated with the posture, practice, and theology of lament, are defined, outlined, and discussed towards the end of this book. Identified as a creative outworking and expression of trust, lament becomes a practice of the people of God that needs to be recovered and remembered.

Lament creates a liminal space in which one recognizes that they live by gift and not by possession, that they are satisfied by relationships of attentive fidelity and not, as Brueggemann suggests, by amassing commodities as

7. Gorman, *Becoming the Gospel*, 53.
8. Van Opstal, *Next Worship*, 63.
9. Clayton, "Bob Lee Killing."
10. Keller, *Generous Justice*, 10.

pseudonym for success.[11] Lament helps one be attentive to God and to others in their community. Lament is an example of trust and hope, directed at and to God, with the intent of bringing restoration and respite, shalom and repair to their context, their grief, and their community. Finally, lament is the first step towards a theopraxis of witness for the people of San Francisco that leads to the redemption and liberation of the city.

11. Brueggemann, *Sabbath as Resistance*, 85.

4

San Francisco
A Case Study

The cool grey city of love...

—George Sterling

Some of the dissonance people in the city of San Francisco experience from the local church and the disconnections associated with its hyper-triumphal, evangelical approach to grief and suffering that emanate from a discord of narratives and subsequent dissonance between the local church and the city it is seeking to serve. This book attempts to bring to light some of the realities of San Francisco, as a case study, and so provide some guidance and insight as to why the City continues to be the least churched city in America. This chapter will also explore how the local church's posture and practice may be contributing to this ongoing reality.

It must be noted that throughout this book, I speak to the complex and nuanced point at hand: there exists within American evangelical Christianity a numb denial of its imperative to lament in moments of crisis and despair. Subsequently, the posture and practice of authentic lament functions as a tool of and for bridge-building, peacemaking, healing, and hope that flows from a place of despair to eventual hope. This enterprise seeks to engage the theology, posture, and practice of lament that connects

14

people with one another and allows communal sharing to truly become redemptive in character.

In this chapter I tackle numerous aspects of the community context of the city of San Francisco. I outline and examine the history and emersion of the city of San Francisco, including its establishment, history, demographics, and cultural characteristics that make it unlike any other city in the United States. I also consider some relevant theological and cultural gaps that exist between the local evangelical church and the city, and the effects associated with the lost language of lament in public and private church-specific spaces. Finally, using current data, I examine the response of lament and its possible implications for a city like San Francisco and lay the foundation as a case study in practical ecclesiology. This approach, it should be stressed, seeks to offer a hermeneutical approach for the local church to engage the city more appropriately, rather than merely being prescriptive—and in doing so make sense of ecclesial footprints of lament forged in the lives of those who follow Jesus in the *cool, gray city of love*.

A Mosaic of Many Expressions

Located on San Francisco Bay, on the western edge of the Bay Area in Northern California, San Francisco is a city of diverse voices, numerous political movements, social activism, progressive beliefs, and the epicenter of tech and innovation. Yet, the city's recent history witnesses a perpetual oscillation between technological innovation and progressive ideologies that sees it caught in a dogmatic limbo that requires a seismic realignment towards greater degrees of care, courage, and vision.

In the first decade of the twentieth century, San Francisco was a small port town on the west coast that was dominated by a small military outpost, the Presidio. Soon after the end of the Mexican–American War, where California was ceded to the United States, businessman James Marshall found gold in Sutter's Mill, California, in 1848—which catalyzed the California gold rush of 1849.

San Francisco was the main port of call for those involved in the Gold Rush. It was the sailing port for those traveling to Northern California by boat or the growing urban epicenter for those traveling over land, via horse and carriage from the East. In the space of two years the population of the city exploded from one thousand residents in 1848 to twenty-five thousand in 1850.

The California gold rush ended in 1855 but San Francisco's impact on the American consciousness did not cease there. The city and the Bay Area continued to be known as the *Gateway to the West* and the city continued to grow both in popularity and importance. At one stage, the influx of immigrants from the Eastern Hemisphere and those by boat was so great, Angel Island, situated north of the city in the North Bay, was colloquially known as the *Ellis Island of the West.*

Popular historian David Talbot, in *Season of the Witch: Enchantment, Terror, and Deliverance in the City of Love,* writes,

> Great cities usually have been founded by wealthy burghers and craftsmen—their spires and monuments a testament to the holiness of their work ethic. But San Francisco's high society was a devil's dinner party, a rogue's crew of robber barons, saloon keepers, and shrew harlots. When the town's painted ladies went to the theater, gentlemen would rise until they were seated. By 1866, there were 31 saloons to every place of worship.[1]

San Francisco was not established like other American cities, as a nod to Eurocentric pilgrims, colonizing an ill-informed promised land and embodying the evil myth of manifest destiny. No—San Francisco was, and still is, the wild frontier outpost known more for its oscillation between progressive and liberal values, its ongoing battle with the outside world within US politics, and its export of European-style social ideas that drive conservative news commentators into a frenzy: universal health care, gay marriage, a living minimal wage, public transport, immigrant sanctuary cities, bicycle-friendly streets, legalized marijuana, and stricter environmental and consumer regulations, just to name a few. This openness to change, social tolerance, and shared sense of humanity is, and has been, indicative of city that holds its patchwork of people together in a mosaic of many expressions.

Having been spared the ravages of the American Civil War, the city benefited from the post-war movement of Americans traveling westward. In 1869, the transcontinental railroad was completed which linked New York City to San Francisco by train. By 1900, San Francisco was a city of over three hundred thousand people, by far the largest city on the West Coast and the eighth largest city in the United States at the time. It was home to some of the largest and most important companies in the world, such as *Wells Fargo Bank, Ghirardelli Chocolate,* and *Levis Straus,* the inventor of denim jeans.

---

1. Talbot, *Season of the Witch,* xv.

San Francisco was also a vast cosmopolitan city with intricate architecture and impressive mansions in flamboyant neighborhoods such Nob Hill, Pacific Heights, and Presidio Heights. This all lent to the foundations of a bohemian culture that still exists today and makes San Francisco one of the top tourist destinations in the United States, visited in the past by such luminary writers as Oscar Wilde, Robert Louis Stevenson, Rudyard Kipling, and Mark Twain. San Francisco was known as the *Paris of the West* and the epicenter of artistic and progressive thought, life, and language on the West Coast. Up until the 1906 earthquake, San Francisco was a larger, more vibrant, and more effervescent city than Seattle, Los Angeles, or San Diego.

The City and the Bay Area have been on the leading edge of wider contextual changes that impact the church and influence the country, that neither can afford to ignore. This area of the United States, from Northern California to the Canadian border in the Pacific Northwest, has been described as a signpost of what the rest of the United States engages with in the following five to seven years. Both Seattle and San Francisco embody a reality that whatever happens becomes concrete in these towns, encroaching upon and infiltrating American culture and worldview within half a generation. San Francisco, simply put, is a canary in the mine.[2] The dynamic nature of this City, for better or for worse, can be grounded in several characteristics that can map out wider developments and trends that feel the ripple-effect of its ideology, universalism, and libertarian pursuits—progressivism, the growth of tech and innovation, urbanization, and post-Christian religious ideologies. These realities look to reshape the United States as an environment for Christian practice and witness in the coming years. San Francisco has a unique role to play in the creative social imaginary of the local church that contributes to its growth, life, and ongoing contextual ecclesiology.

A Failed City?

As the city emerged from the COVID-19 pandemic, it found itself in a quagmire of juxtaposing moments. Nellie Bowles, in a landmark article from *The Atlantic* titled "How San Francisco Became a Failed City: And How it Could Recover," writes,

> I used to tell myself that San Francisco's politics were wacky, but the city was trying—really trying—to be good. But the reality is

2. James, *Church Planting*, 110.

that with the smartest minds and so much money and the very best of intentions, San Francisco became a cruel city. It became so dogmatically progressive that maintaining the purity of the politics required accepting—or at least ignoring—devastating results.[3]

During the pandemic, more people died in San Francisco from drug overdoses than the virus itself.[4] San Franciscans are careful to use language that centers a person's humanity—one does not say a homeless person. Instead, one says a person experiencing homelessness. Despite such centering language, San Francisco has become a city where people die on the sidewalk, fentanyl has emerged as its own pandemic, homelessness remains on the city's biggest concerns, and legislation around crime has found the city divided down economic, geographic, and racial lines. In early 2023, San Francisco made headlines for the public murder of a tech executive and ongoing violence throughout the city. Blending empathy-driven progressivism with California libertarianism, this approach to crime, drug use, COVID-19, and homelessness was becoming distinctly San Franciscan.

Global in name and stature, San Francisco is a mosaic of local communities and personalities. The city consists of thirty-six neighborhoods embodying various distinct and dynamic personalities. This mosaic includes areas such as the Castro, known for its reception and early acceptance of the LGBTQIA+ community; Chinatown which, post–gold rush in 1849, became the largest Chinese community settled outside East and South-East Asia; Haight-Ashbury, synonymous with 1967's Summer of Love movement and hippie culture that continues to this day; Fillmore District, originally the epicenter for black excellence and jazz on the west coast, the nature of the Fillmore changed with redlining and economics; and the East Cut, San Francisco's newest neighborhood as a result of gentrification and designed to be delineated from FiDi (the Financial District), SOMA (South of Market), South Park, South Beach, and the Embarcadero as the city's newest urban residential quarter—purely for profit.

The city expresses itself in many ways and, as a result, many find it difficult to describe San Francisco's culture as one, unified quality. Underneath its beauty and striking position on the Bay and its position at the mouth of the Golden Gate, San Francisco holds within its arms a city of grief and despair.

3. Nellie Bowles, "How San Francisco Became," para. 14.
4. Nellie Bowles, "How San Francisco Became," para. 23.

The City and Grief

Acclaimed America writer, playwright, and poet George Sterling, describing San Francisco, coined the phrase "The Cool, Grey City of Love."[5] Like San Francisco, Sterling was an eccentric collection of paradoxes. In an article by the *San Francisco Chronicle*, in October 2020, he was described as "extremely sociable but deeply solitary, a compulsive womanizer who found his deepest fulfillment in friendships with men, a Dionysian reveler who was profoundly modest, a gifted poet who did not take his muse seriously and needed the stimulation of alcohol or sex to prod himself into creativity."[6] What makes San Francisco so captivating to those on the inside—those who call it home—and those on the outside, the critics, tourists, and political commentators, is this juxtaposition of beauty and grief. San Francisco embodies a bizarre binary that has captivated people for almost two hundred years yet witnessed the city struggle as it seeks to fulfill its potential as the Paris of the West. This cool, grey city of love has become a cold, broken city of grief. The city that was the epicenter for the 1967 Summer of Love, has given way to a city that is caught in its own winter of discontent.

San Francisco is in a current crisis of disorder. Be it a lack of affordable housing, rising low-range criminal activity, homelessness, the fentanyl crisis, mental health concerns, or the tech exodus, San Francisco is in a state of decay. Michael Schellenberger, from *The Spectator*—a British weekly newsmagazine framed around politics, current affairs, and culture—writes,

> Many of the problems [in San Francisco have] stemmed from Covid-19. California's prisons, jails and homeless shelters were under orders to reduce their occupancy. But none of these problems started with the pandemic. Between 2008 and 2019, about 18,000 companies, including Toyota, Charles Schwab and Hewlett-Packard fled California due to a constellation of problems sometimes summarized as "poor business climate." California has the highest income tax, highest gasoline tax and highest sales tax

---

5. George Sterling's poem describes the City at war and in tension with itself. Sterling describes a city of beauty and grace, yet one of pity and darkness. The City (a phrase coined by the now relocated Golden State Warriors who recently moved from Oakland back to San Francisco) is one of beauty yet sorrow. Splendor yet burden. Attraction yet trouble. Post-pandemic, San Francisco has found itself at a moment of grief, struggling with homelessness, falling commercial occupancy rates, rising house prices, and a shrinking city. It is a city of irony and juxtaposition. Beauty, yet pain and grief and one the Sterling's poem frames so well, the cool, gray city of love.

6. Gary Kamiya, "SF's Unofficial Port Laureate," para. 2.

in the United States, spends significantly more than other states on homelessness, and yet has worse outcomes.[7]

This decline and decay is not a new phenomenon to the city. Narrowing in on the mental health crisis that permeates the city and is a correlation to San Francisco's homeless issues, Schellenberger writes, "The crisis of untreated mental illness, addiction and homelessness is growing worse. Between 2013 and 2016, complaints of homeless encampments to San Francisco's 311 line rose from two per day to 63 per day."[8] Stellenberger continues,

> Between 2005 and 2020, the estimated number of homeless people in San Francisco increased from 5,404 to 8,124. The estimated number of unsheltered homeless rose from 2,655 to 5,180. The San Francisco Bay Area as a whole saw sheltered and unsheltered homeless increase by 32 per cent between 2015 and 2020, with the share of unsheltered homeless rising from 65 to 73 per cent. The total more than doubled in Alameda County, which includes Oakland and Berkeley, between 2015 and 2020.[9]

Comparing San Francisco and the other proximal cities in the Bay Area, it must be noted that nationwide homelessness "fell from 763,000 to 568,000 between 2005 and 2020. In the same 15-year period, the homeless populations of leading cities in America such as Chicago, Greater Miami and Greater Atlanta declined 19 per cent, 32 per cent, and 43 per cent respectively."[10]

Grief is the emotional wave that knocks any person off their feet. Done well, grief can be a form of learning and a form of connecting, that with support, can guide and shape and inform. Without resources and in the absence of community, grief becomes paralyzing. It is a reality and a crisis that can on the one hand take the wind out of a person while, on the other hand, leave someone defeated, broken, disconnected, and lifeless. The social complexities embedded in the current collective fabric of San Francisco are legitimately overwhelming and crushing for those suffering in isolation on the city streets. Despite San Francisco's progressive and well-informed intentions, those suffering and grieving need more support. The first step to a resolution and solution is lamenting the current realties of the

---

7. Shellenberger, "San Francisco is Decaying," para. 2.
8. Shellenberger, "San Francisco is Decaying," para. 7.
9. Shellenberger, "San Francisco is Decaying," para. 10.
10. Shellenberger, "San Francisco is Decaying," para. 11.

city and in doing so finding common ground with those who are suffering and grieving in isolation.

San Francisco and Lament

San Francisco is an anxious city. "The budget to tackle homelessness and provide supportive housing has been growing exponentially for years. In 2021, the city announced that it would pour more than $1 billion into the issue over the next two years. But almost 8,000 people remain on the streets."[11] The presence of lament as a posture and practice of worship in gospel-centered, Spirit-led communities provides the opportunity to influence, transform, and liberate a city like San Francisco.

The practice of lament is countercultural to most people in the North American evangelical church.[12] Lament brings with it a transformative, liminal space that recognizes God as the creator and author of all things, that God wants to hear and know our pain, and can handle anything people send God's way. Lament, functioning as a boundary and practiced as a tool of worship, is the first fundamental practice that would aid the faith leaders of the church in San Francisco toward a posture and practice of communal grieving, healing, and restoration. Yet, if the people of God refuse to lament in moments of grief and sorrow, it cuts them off not only from one another, but also from God. Card affirms that "this same failure to lament also hampers us in being able to fully know and reach out to the poor, who Jesus told us were to be our central concern."[13] Card continues, "How can we speak to the suffering and poor if we do not learn their language, the language of lament? Until we learn to honestly embrace our hopelessness and theirs, there will be no true gospel to be heard. Until we learn to lament, we have nothing to say to most of the world."[14] This is not only a question of language, but also an exploration of differing narratives. It is a central tenant of this book that of this paper that without lament the people of God cannot cultivate common ground with those suffering in their city. Without lament one's personal or communal narrative cannot be reimagined and formed deeply with and by God. The evangelical church currently speaks a different language and embodies a divergent narrative

11. Bowles, "How San Francisco Became," para. 21.

12. Rah, *Prophetic Lament*.

13. Card, *Sacred Sorrow*, 29.

14. Card, *Sacred Sorrow*, 26.

to those they are trying (and called to) reach in the name of Jesus. Without lament, evangelical faith communities run the risk of having a thin, veiled, and dissonant connection with the city.

Transformation begins with God. Acknowledging what God is doing and paying attention to God's Spirit is a skill that can be cultivated. It is the role of the leader in a faith community to consider what God is doing in this city, in this moment. Prior to the pandemic, the leadership of a number San Francisco churches predominately only had the language of victory. As the pandemic became a more serious reality for many, senior leaders and pastors became increasingly silent. They were not trained nor prepared to engage directly with the emotional grief and suffering experienced by many in their congregations. The Old Testament encourages the fullest expression of what it means to be human—including the practice and tradition of lament. Jesus will bless those who do (Luke 6:21). When grief is encountered during this time, most leaders were silent. Lament was part of the theological vernacular.

Psalm 55 gives one an insight into the necessity of and narrative arc associated with lament. It is a narrative arc that brings with it peace, assurance, and trust. To lament is a peacemaking activity with oneself and one's context because the practice of lamenting involves God in the process. In verse 1, the psalmist writes, "Give ear to my prayer, O God; do not hide yourself from my supplication." In this moment of grief and pain, the writer is seeking after God with the desire that he actively and intentionally intervenes in their moment of pain. As the reality of their pain becomes more evident, the writer shifts from supplication to worry. The psalmist asserts in verse 5, "Fear and trembling come upon me, and horror overwhelms me." The gravity of their grief has become debilitating, almost crushing.

I wonder, when was the last time you found yourself in a moment where your grief felt like it was crushing you? How did you respond? What words or actions did you offer up to God? Did you ask him to take it away? Did you question why he was allowing you to go through such pain? Did not the God of peace and joy promise to keep you from affliction?

It is common misnomer that many have assumed that scripture tells us that God promises to protect and save us from any and all forms of grief, pain, or calamity. This is simply not true. God never promises to save us *from* pain, grief, despair, or suffering. He does, however, promise to save and sustain us *through* our pain, grief, despair, or suffering. I've come to see that as we lament and actively throw our burdens and grief on him that God and his Spirit becomes a tangible, non-anxious presence.

The psalmist in Ps 55 offers us an insight to the reality and power of lament. In verses 22 and 23, they write, "Cast your burden on the LORD, and he will sustain you; he will never permit the righteous to be moved. But you, O God, will cast them down into the lowest pit; the bloodthirsty and treacherous shall not live out half their days. But I will trust in you." To lament to God and grieve your pain is not to merely a practice of venting, but of trust and hope, believing deeply—by giving God all your pain and emotion and frustration—that God can and will meet you in your dirge and comfort you, even though he may remain silent. Silence is not a symbol of one's absence. No. Silence allows the suffering voice to speak in the midst of ruins and so create a space that recognizes God is present in all things, even pain. Lament, ironically, creates space for a non-anxious presence and so seeks to recognizes the presence of God in all things.

San Francisco is a city in pain. Pithy platitudes and common sayings of hope have silenced the suffering voice of those subject to its pain. I wonder how the people of San Francisco would respond if the people of God, on mission with God, returned and remembered the practice of lament. To be missional in this way provide space for people to reflect, remember, and articulate their pain and grief to God as holy first-step towards hope, wholeness, and shalom.

Moral Injury

Without practicing lament as a form of personal self-care, communal liminal transformation, or intentionally creating space for trust and peace-making in one's life, faith leaders in a city like San Francisco run the risk of imposing unhealthy practices on well-meaning and well-intentioned platitudes on the followers of Jesus in the form of moral injury.

Moral injury is what happens when one's shared habits or norms become violent to others. Chanequa Walker-Barnes writes, "Moral injury is the failure to live in accordance with our deepest moral aspirations and as the diminishment that comes from our own actions as well as the actions of those against us."[15] Moral injury can take the form of living outside a context that brings for affirmation, healthy boundaries, safe contexts of expression, and ultimately brave spaces of shared belonging where individuals

15. Walker-Barnes. *I Bring the Voices*, 126.

not only believe intellectually and philosophically that they can express moments of pain, and grief, and so be vulnerable with and to those they do life with—like a local faith community—but also practice it concretely.

This is part of the complexity of local churches and local faith leaders. There seems to be personal and collective dissonance within the evangelical community around concrete practices of lament. Church leaders and pastors may philosophically affirm such practices, but when the "rubber hits the road" many seem to feel and believe that if they do share their pain and grievances from the pulpit or the platform that it will harm their ministry. This may speak to why many believe that they is a direct correlation (or even worse, a causation) between their ability to believe *that the best is yet to come*, and the size of their church ministry. As a result, despite what many may believe intellectually, to be vulnerable does not mean to lament or show one's faith. Vulnerability is equated with doubt, weakness, and disbelief, the antithesis of a hyper-individualistic, hyper-wealthy, hyper-triumphal, hyper-victorious way of following Jesus.

Such a posture and practice then, becomes disingenuous to those walking with pain and enduring suffering. When people in evangelical faith communities and cities like San Francisco find that they are unable to speak or express their pain in such settings, they lose their ability to connect and cultivate belonging.

Moral injury, then, becomes the common reality for those who say they're *hurt by the church*. In reality, it was not an inanimate object or broad, vague group people who hurt them, it was one unintentional interaction where a person misspoke or transferred a pithy platitude that failed to resonate with the pain and suffering another had shared.

When the church fails to lament but, instead, embodies north American evangelical norm framed around a hyper-individualistic, hyper-wealthy, hyper-triumphal, hyper-victorious way of following Jesus, they impose a toxic shared habit or norm that has subsequently become violent to others. They have imposed a moral injury.

It is imperative and urgent, therefore, that the faith leaders within the city of San Francisco seek to create a culture of lament, trust, peacemaking, and joy by demonstrating and embodying the missional creative praxis of lament that is a lost gift designed as a trust-building form of worship for those who say they follow Jesus, and a practice that is transformative for both the individual and communal follower of Jesus.

5

Lament

A Contextual Response

One's first question should never be 'what must I do,' instead,
the first right question needs to be, 'who must I become'?

—BEN MCBRIDE

THE CITY OF SAN Francisco, with all its complexities, beauty, grief, and struggle requires a contextual response. The evangelical phenomenon has witnessed the rise of the McDonaldization[1] of church communities in

1. Originally penned in 1993, George Ritzer, in *The McDonaldization of Society*, speaks of the values and practices that have cultivated fast food and franchising in the US. Values such as control, predictability, efficiency, and calculability have seeped into the way evangelical church movements and organizations have built and framed their Sunday experience. Hillsong is not immune to or alone in this diagnosis. In 2000, author John Drane, in *The McDonaldization of the Church*, doubles down on this reality that permeates American culture and its embedded influence in and on the church. Although not central to this paper, the McDonaldization of the evangelical church could play a central role as to why the practice, liturgy, and art of lament has vacated North American evangelical theology. It also speaks to and plays a part in people inability to respond well to and be formed by grief. The practice of lament breaks through the reality of the McDonaldization of evangelical theology and helps people navigate their individual and communal grief and sorrow in a more specific, contextual, and culturally relevant way. One could go a step further and say that lament is the key tool God has given the people of God to think well theologically and say embody a thicker Jesus in all areas of life—especially grief and sorrow.

North America. This phenomenon and narrative simply fail to respond effectively to the theological nuances imperative to a sound, missional, effective, and impactful response that is required for a city like San Francisco, California. Rah writes, in *A Prophetic Lament: A Call for Justice in Troubled Times*, "A triumphant and success-oriented narrative limits the twenty-first-century American evangelical theological imagination. The narrative of triumph silences a narrative of suffering."[2] He continues, "The narrative of suffering and the lament that accompanies suffering [helps the people of God] . . . move towards an acknowledgement of who is in charge."[3] Lament allows the people of God to slow down, wait, trust, and see what God is doing in the midst of pain. To lament calls God into the work, asking God to be proximal to us and God's people, as one navigates through the deluge of heartache with little-to-no perceived vision of hope or justice.

Lament is a way of equipping and supporting the people of God, on mission with God, in San Francisco towards a healthy and human way of responding to the fentanyl crisis in the city. It needs to also be seen and understood as a more appropriate and healthy way of discerning how to respond to the cost of housing and chronic homelessness. It is imperative that the people of God, on mission with God, in San Francisco see and understand lament as a tool of restoration and hope in a city that witnesses much hopelessness. They need to lament.

Lament needs to be first response because it is an act of trust, hope, and imagination when all seems lost. Lament reimagines the narrative of God's capacity to form and reform a community of people, helping to form a fuller more appropriate response to grief and injustice and despair. Emmanuel Katongole writes in *Born from Lament: The Theology and Politics of Hope in Africa*, "What emerges is a comprehensive vision of lament as a complex set of practices or disciplines—a way of seeing, standing, and wrestling or arguing with God, and thus a way hoping in the midst of ruins . . . a way of [contextually] turning in and toward to God in the midst of suffering."[4]

Katongole emphasizes that there is a God who is able to respond to the excess of evil with an excess of love. This pushes the people of God on mission with God in San Francisco to a theopraxis of witness and so a passionate advocacy with, for, and on behalf of those who cannot contend for themselves. Lament helps to eventually shift people out of a context of denial where unhealthy practices tend to grow and cultivate that ultimately fail to

2. Rah, *Prophetic Lament*, 72.

3. Rah, *Prophetic Lament*, 72.

4. Katongole, *Born from Lament*, xvii.

engage directly with the pain at hand. The absence of lament, in season of deep pain and despair, is akin to believing that one is living their best life in the presence of a broken leg, severe concussion, or amputated limb.

To be clear, the pursuit of the practice of lament in one's life is not anti-happiness. The presence of lament is anti-forced happiness. If lament is not part of the equation of someone's processing engagement with grief with God, it often results in problematic long-term symptoms of one's faith. These symptoms may include cheap joy, forced celebration, or possibly a thin veneer of hope. Lament is imperative to the advocacy of the city and is synonymous with the people of God. Lament is an apolitical, theological practice that seeks the flourishing of all people.

Embracing the Other

Theologian Miroslav Volf points out that loving, knowing, and embracing the other—the one who does not think, act, speak, or engage *as I do*—is the only fitting response to the love of the cross. Volf writes, "When God sets out to embrace the enemy, the result is the cross . . . . Having been embraced by God, we must make space for others in ourselves and invite them in—even our enemies. This is what we enact as we celebrate the Eucharist. In receiving Christ's broken body and spilled blood, we, in a sense, receive all those whom Christ received by suffering."[5] This shift will seek to implement the imperative of a new creative, missional, social imaginary that recovers, renews, and reimagines the philosophy, posture, and practice of Hillsong in San Francisco. This will be explored by discussing three themes: (i) history and context; (ii) the nuances of Hillsong San Francisco; and (iii) the common refrain, *the best is yet to come.*

Hillsong California

Hillsong San Francisco sits in a unique position within Hillsong California. Hillsong San Francisco is one of three campuses—the others being Hillsong Los Angeles (LA) and Hillsong Orange County (OC)—within the Hillsong California model. This centralized hub-and-spoke model, that functionally and practically makes most of its strategic decisions from LA, cultivates a narrative within the ecclesial expression of its community that fosters minimal agency or autonomy in directing and devising its missional strategy.

5. Volf, *Exclusion and Embrace*, 129.

What this means is that Hillsong San Francisco has little-to-no creative agency to creatively contextualize its missional philosophy, posture, and practice specific for the city of San Francisco and the greater Bay Area.

This becomes problematic when one recognizes the different missional, practical, theological, and hermeneutical needs of both cities. San Francisco is not Los Angeles. To exegete, interpret, and so respond effectively to the needs of the city of San Francisco requires greater agency and flexibility. This is simply not possible with a centralized hub-and-spoke model. An evangelical megachurch, like Hillsong California, is not alone in using this model. It is fairly common amongst evangelical churches that seek to church plant, replicate, and impose a franchise approach to their church growth model.

As one reads this part of the book, it is imperative to remember that the purpose of this chapter is to frame a philosophy, posture, and practice—essentially a theopraxis of formation and witness—of lament examining Hillsong California and the city of San Francisco as a case study for other churches and church leaders. By embracing this new, creative, and reimagined practice, it is hoped Hillsong San Francisco will explore what it possibly means to be less myopic and service-centric in its mission and so become the *sent ones* embracing the *other*.

History and Context

Founded in 1983 as Hills Christian Life Centre, a Pentecostal church in the northwestern suburbs of Sydney, Australia, with some roots in Baptist and Salvation Army traditions, Hillsong Church has experienced a convoluted and contentious history in recent years. Hillsong describes itself as "a contemporary Christian church. Overwhelmed by the gift of salvation we have found in Jesus, we have a heart for authentic worship, are passionate about the local church, and on mission to see God's kingdom established on earth." Since the early 1980s Hillsong has grown to a network of churches found in thirty cities through the world, with an average weekly attendance of 150,000 people.[6]

Operating as *Hills Christian Life Centre* for twenty-six years, the church changed its name in 2001 to Hillsong Church. Tanya Riches writes, "This name [Hillsong Church] was previously reserved for its musical product, distributed, and marketed as *Hillsongs* by HMA [Hillsong Music Australia]. Early on, the decision was made to emphasize the church as

6. "About Hillsong."

the artist—fusing the identity of the organization with its music."[7] Former global senior pastor and founder, Brian Houston, explains this in an interview televised on *Australian Story*,

> Hillsong was originally the name of our music and the church was called Hills Christian Life Centre, but people used to talk about "that Hillsong Church" and the name Hillsong actually became famous, if you like, around the world. So, in the end, we thought, that's what we're known as, so we became Hillsong Church.[8]

Founded upon a vision of "a healthy church, changing lives through Christ,"[9] Hillsong has found itself in the crosshairs of controversy since the end of the pandemic. Most well-known for its worship music, which can be found in the church services of many evangelical faith communities, Hillsong Music is global juggernaut. Worship songs include "The Power of Your Love," "Shout to the Lord," "What a Beautiful Name," "Mighty to Save," "Hosanna," and "God is Able" (to name a few). Hillsong in the United States is more well known for its worship music than it is being a local church.[10]

Hillsong's pursuit of embedding itself in the Sunday services of many evangelical churches was and has been on the forefront of its mission and vision since the early 1990s. Currently, Hillsong Music has three main ministries: Hillsong Worship, Hillsong United, and Young and Free. Through these ministries the church has released more than sixty-five albums, 550 songs, has been nominated for numerous Grammy Music Awards, in 2016 was named the Top Christian Artist at the Billboard Music Awards, and in 2018 Hillsong Worship received a Grammy Award for Best Contemporary Christian Song/Performance with their song "What a Beautiful Name."[11] No wonder people in the United States and other parts of the world that are not privy to the church's Australian context and are ignorant of its humble, local church beginnings.

Describing Hillsong's emphasis on and around worship music, Kelsey McKinney from *The Fader* writes, "Every Hillsong service plays songs produced in-house by one of the church's three different musical entities: Hillsong Worship, for church services; the touring act Hillsong United; and the youth-focused Young and Free. All three are nestled under the church's

---

7. Riches and Wagner, "Evolution of Hillsong Music," 21.

8. Jones, *Australian Story*, "Life of Brian."

9. "About Hillsong."

10. McGinnis, "Should We Keep Singing Hillsong?"

11. "About Hillsong."

Hillsong Music label."[12] In a paper titled *The Evolution of Hillsong Music*, Tanya Riches and Tom Wagner write,

> The ubiquity of its music in evangelical (and, increasingly, non-evangelical) churches is largely due to annual music releases marketed as specialized Christian resources. On any given Sunday, worship songs penned by Hillsong songwriters can be heard in churches worldwide. Hillsong has sold over 11 million albums and garnered over 50 gold and platinum awards.[13]

McKinney continues, "The church [Hillsong] gives any church or place of worship permission to play or perform Hillsong's music as an act of worship without paying a performance copyright which means anywhere around the world, a Hillsong song can be played for free with the lyrics projected on a screen. That's great for Hillsong's mission and for business."[14] Yet, people forget that Hillsong started as a local church.

Hillsong first entered the United States in 2010, when it opened *Hillsong New York City*. From that moment, the church sought to reimagine people's perception and understanding of God by not simply trying to do church, but by bringing a youthful and attractive model of church to the city, centered around its worship. A model of church undergirded by narratives of *triumphalism*, *wealth*, *prosperity*, and *overcoming*. Since its inauguration in New York City and expansion to become Hillsong East Coast, the Hillsong brand of churches grew around the United States to include congregations in Kansas City, Missouri; Dallas, Texas; and Boston, Massachusetts. Hillsong California started life in 2014 under the leadership of Ben Houston.[15] Yet, despite its growth and popularity, Hillsong continues to have mixed success in the United States.

In 2016, Hillsong San Francisco—established as a church plant out of Hillsong Los Angeles—started organically with the unique purpose of growing community and becoming a relational presence in San Francisco.[16] By the end of 2017, Hillsong San Francisco was rooted in the community with twenty-seven connect groups, engaging over 650 people, with more than 380 people attending weekly.[17] On the back of Hillsong's global success

12. McKinney. "How Hillsong Church Conquered," para. 5.

13. Riches and Wagner, "Evolution of Hillsong Music," 21.

14. McKinney, "How Hillsong Church Conquered," para. 37.

15. Riches and Wagner, "Evolution of Hillsong Music," 37.

16. Houston, "Announcement: Hillsong San Francisco."

17. Statistics regarding attendance around connect groups and church services are

as a worship band and Hillsong's growing influence in other cities in the United States, such as New York City, and Los Angeles, planting a church in San Francisco seemed like the right next move.

Fast-forward to the end of 2019, Hillsong San Francisco was located in August Hall on Mason Street, in heart of downtown San Francisco. Sundays consisted of three services at 10:00 a.m., 12:00 p.m., and 6:00 p.m. with close to 1,500 people in attendance. The leadership had changed, as had its focus and locus from 2016. Hillsong San Francisco embodied a service-centric approach to church with a heavy focus on Sunday attendance and alter-call responses. The church's social justice ministry arm, Hillsong City Care,[18] played a key role in connecting the church community with other social service initiatives within the boundaries of the city of San Francisco, including City Team, Mobilize Love, and City Eats, to name a few. But their main mission was building and growing Sunday services.

As the COVID-19 pandemic became a reality and the mayor of San Francisco, London Breed, executed the city's stay-at-home order, Hillsong San Francisco—like many other churches in the city and the United States—moved swiftly to online services. The impact of the pandemic was instantaneous. Social distancing measures and the reality of screen fatigue became hurdles for many faith communities as they attempted to maintain interpersonal connections and cultivate community in that shadow of this deadly contagion.

Moving to online services was not a radical move. Frank Newport writes,

> The abrupt cessation of in-person worship in churches . . . around the country is one of the most significant *sudden* disruptions in the practice of religion in U.S. history. But "virtual" worship is certainly not a new concept in this country. For almost a century, religious entities have been using "new" methods of communication to reach vast audiences—first radio, then television; and, in recent years, well before the current COVID-19 virus crisis, online technologies.[19]

---

rounded down to maintain conservative estimates as numbers were not recorded consistently prior to the COVID-19 pandemic. Names, roles, and descriptions will be kept anonymous as a means of maintaining confidentiality. Numbers are only shared to demonstrate themes associated with missional philosophy and praxis. Cultivating church community in San Francisco is a difficult process and one that, in the context of this book, is not taken lightly.

18. "City Care."

19. Newport, "Religion and the COVID-19 Virus," para. 2.

Hillsong San Francisco, like other churches who had the resources to do so, adapted to this *new normal*. Yet, if the COVID-19 pandemic showed anything across the United States and many part of global, western evangelicalism, it was the lack of social imagination and creative missional praxis of the local church to the grief and sorrow many were experiencing both to the pandemic and the racial powder keg that the violent, racialized murder of George Floyd. Hillsong San Francisco, like many other North American evangelical church communities, could not speak to the grief, loss, sorrow, or pain that many people were experiencing from social isolation to racial anger to the death of friends and family members, or to the loss of employment, housing, or lifestyle. Virtual services became the new version of radio or TV. It was televangelism by another medium.

Hillsong San Francisco's faith leaders, like many pastors and faith leaders who could not meet in-person due to relative social-distancing protocols imposed by local cities and counties, grappled with the reality and narratives of being relevant, present, and faithful in a moment where the law did not allow people to gather together in the name of Christ. What did it mean and what could it look like to be faithful a presence in the lives of those in one's local community? Do they form intentional social bubbles? Do members of the local church limit their social interactions to a more localized social reality?

David Fitch, in *Faithful Presence: Seven Disciplines That Shape the Church for Mission*, touches on this reality when he writes,

> Faithful presence must therefore be a communal reality before it can infect the world. It must take shape as a whole way of life in a people. From this social space we infect the world for change. Here we give witness to the kingdom breaking in and invite the world to join in. For this to happen, however, we need a set of disciplines that shape Christians into such communities in the world.[20]

To be present and faithful and missionally creative during the pandemic, let alone pre- or post-lockdown, requires leaders to think critically, creatively, contextually, and divergently. The people of God, on mission with God, are required to exegete their local suburb, village, town, or city and so respond faithfully to the needs of the people around them. This was not the case for Hillsong San Francisco. The church struggled to maintain its relevance during the pandemic and basically resorted to its service-centric philosophy via YouTube live streams from Southern California. Hillsong San Francisco

20. Fitch. *Faithful Presence*, 14.

struggled to be missionally creative during the pandemic and was unable to navigate how to be the church for the city of San Francisco without in-person services.

A Double Pandemic

This double-pandemic moment—of COVID-19 and the racial powder keg of the murder of George Floyd and the Black Lives Matter movement—showcased the extent to which the North American evangelical community needed the theology and practice of lament. The quick responses of many evangelical churches who previously remained silent, absent, or disengaged around racial bias or systemic racism immediately became self-identified experts in the field. Although well intended and well-meaning, evangelical church leaders, including those who were leading Hillsong Australia, Hillsong California, Hillsong San Francisco, and Hillsong New York City, were guilty of moving too fast as they attempted to lead the conversation and practice of systemic racism, racial bias, and racial reconciliation. Yet, if they had slowed down, taken a breath, and made their first step into this double-pandemic space one of lament, many of these church leaders would have responded more appropriately.

Ben McBride, a social activists and community builder from Oakland, California, affirms, "All too often we find ourselves asking the wrong first question. When pressured by expediency and the pursuit of relevance, often as 'what must I do,' instead, the first right question needs to be, 'who must I become'?"[21] White evangelical faith communities, with the ongoing narratives and pursuit of relevance, triumphalism, and wealth were asking themselves a different question. When one asks themselves, "Who must I become?" they're opening themselves to a new way of being, a new narrative and new paradigm of seeing and so, eventually, engaging with and in local spaces and places. It is a process of self-reflection that is ongoing, dynamic, and reflexive. To lament in the face of one's own or another's pain is part of that process of asking the better first right question, *who must I become?*

To lament in the moment of the COVID-19 pandemic and the racial uprising and lament of the murder of George Floyd is to participate with God and be willing to let go of one's predetermined and preconceived ideas of *doing*. To lament is to protest at and with God a deep dirge of despair and, so, be willing for God to enter into your pain and frustration. To lament in

21. McBride, *Troubling the Water*, 9.

these moments is to let the suffering voice speak. Creating space for those who hear the tears and suffering transform one's being and so be open to who God is asking us to become and how the Spirit of God wants to engage in that moment.

Natasha Sistrunk Robinson in *Voices of Lament: Reflections on Brokenness and Hope in a World Longing for Justice*, writes,

> I grieve the toxic environment of performance allyship and a weightless solidarity that social media has allowed out culture to create. The urgent, knee-jerk response is always in the moment to appear relevant, "woke," or socially conscious. Real leadership and social change take long-term commitments, strategy, and planning, and the investments of resources and time. I'm looking for a people of goodwill to make a long-term commitment to justice, love, and truth-telling.[22]

The city of San Francisco needed the people of God to lament with it as a practice of *proximity* and *faithfulness*. As homelessness and unemployment rose during the pandemic and as people grieved for their safety, the city needed a community that was willing to see their pain and sit with them, in the midst of ruins. Calling on God to help and guide and protect, just like the psalms of lament, the book of Jeremiah, and the book of Lamentations throughout Scripture demonstrate. Hillsong San Francisco found this all too difficult—hence the need for lament to be refound and centered as part of its theology and practice.

Post-pandemic it has become evident that little had changed missionally and the local church, as a community, needed to engage with lament as a tool of bridge-building, peacemaking, and articulating a *thicker* Jesus. The only effective tool in its ecclesial toolbox was in-person services. David Fitch argues that "faithful presence names the reality that God is present in the world and that he uses a people faithful to his presence to make himself concrete and real amid the world's struggles and pain."[23] Attendance has continued to drop since in-person services restarted. Numbers post-pandemic sit consistently between 120 to 130 people, with one service on a Sunday morning. The location of church has changed from downtown San Francisco to Treasure Island, in the middle of the Bay, distal from community and separated geographically from the city it is called to serve.

22. Robinson. *Voices of Lament*, 20.
23. Fitch, *Faithful Presence*, 10.

6

The Best Is Yet to Come?

The narrative of triumph silences a narrative of suffering

—Prof. Soong-Chang Rah

Axioms have a growing frequency in North American evangelical faith communities. Be it small quips or sayings full of alliteration, axioms have grown in the church as a useful tool, exercised by many evangelical speakers as a communication tool for their congregation. An axiom is known to be a tenet or principle or phrase that people deem to be true. Merriam-Webster defines axiom as "a statement accepted as true as the basis for argument or inference; an established rule or principle or a self-evident truth; a maxim widely accepted for its intrinsic merit."[1]

In 2008, Bill Hybels, founding and former senior pastor of Willow Creek Community Church in the northwest suburbs of Chicago, wrote a book titled *Axiom: Powerful Leadership Proverbs*. In it he writes, "Great leaders not only lead well but are able to articulate in short, memorable phrases how they do so."[2] While there are elements of truth where axioms help communicate and simplify complex realities of life, the risk many evangelical leaders may find themselves in has been framed around oversimplifying and reducing people's convoluted experiences, theology, and

1. "Axiom."
2. Hybels, *Axiom*, 11.

their way of living when it comes to following Jesus. This is in contrast to Scripture, which is typically not about catch phrases or short pithy sayings.

Being a follower of the way of Jesus Christ cannot only be contained within a series of axiomatic beliefs or phrases. Being human and following Jesus is full of lived, theological, and ecclesial complexities that make the Christian life challenging. One such phrase that was made famous by Frank Sinatra's 1964 album, *It Might as Well Be Swing*, is the axiom *the best is yet to come*. Since Hillsong's establishment in the early 1980s and rise to international popularity in the early 2000s, this phrase became a culture truth and phrase attributed with the Hillsong Church and its founding and former global senior pastor, Brian Houston.

The phrase was intended to frame hope, Godly intention, and direction, yet it had been bundled together in a quagmire of prosperity-gospel, hyper-capitalism, and a profound disconnection with the reality of grief and suffering. In his book *Live Love Lead: Your Best is Yet to Come*, Houston writes,

> After seeing the way God changes hearts, meets impossible needs, heals incurable diseases, and restores people, I am convinced beyond a doubt that God didn't create us to live mediocre, settle-for-less lives. He sent his Son to die on a cross so that we could be forgiven and have eternal life, and not so we could sleepwalk through life as we wait for Heaven. The Word of God shows us how to navigate the inevitable twists and turns, and bumps and bruises we may encounter. God has a unique purpose and plan for you—your life, love, and leadership journey was crafted in Heaven long before the foundations of the earth. Your spiritual adventure has already started—and the best is yet to come.[3]

While well-intentioned and full of hope, Houston's axiomatic approach embodies a perceived privilege and exceptionalism that is synonymous with those who either ignore or are ignorant to the book of Lamentations, the Psalms of lament, Job's repeated petitions to God, or Jeremiah's lament of the city of Jerusalem. Such axioms bring with it a narrow *social and prophetic imagination* that is currently synonymous with North American evangelical churches, for which Hillsong Church needs to be included.

Such a narrow social and prophetic imagination fails to appreciate the nuance and complexity of suffering and grief in the life of the people of God. It brings with it a oversimplified, victorious, and jubilant oriented theological and ecclesial posture and practice that becomes blind to and so

---

3. Houston. *Live Love Lead*, 4.

ignores the reality of suffering in the world. Rah writes, "A triumphant and success-oriented narrative limits the twenty-first-century American evangelical theological imagination. The narrative of triumph silences a narrative of suffering."[4] He continues, "The dismantling of privilege requires a disavowal of any pretense of exceptionalism."[5] It is the pretense and practice of such theological exceptionalism, woven with a toxicity that was *manifest destiny*, that one could argue is synonymous with American evangelical theology. This has been evident since the European settlement of the United States that had contributed to this restricted social and prophetic imagination that can only be found in the formative milieu of lament, grief, and suffering.[6]

The phrase "the best is yet to come" weaves within itself a rejection of and ignorance to the imperative of suffering and Godly-forming events. Boxed within the health-wealth gospel and the strands of materialism and capitalism, such a narrative rarely allows space for the problem of pain or a people's grief and loss. God gave to practicing Judeo-Christians the tradition of lament as a deeply liturgical, formative, and prophetic practice that contributes to the expansion of an individual's and community's social imaginary and prophetic imagination. Consequently, the recognition of lament as an imperative practice of worship forms the people of God to become more like Jesus as they engage with the complexities of life in

---

4. Rah, *Prophetic Lament*, 72.

5. Rah, *Prophetic Lament*, 72.

6. Mark Charles and Soong-Chan Rah write, in *Unsettling Truths: The Ongoing Dehumanizing Legacy of the Doctrine of Discovery*, "The Western Theological Imagination was rooted in the assumption of white superiority and the elevation of white flesh. White American Christians have made their own bodies the standard reference in the determination of values and norms, and so whiteness has become universalized and held up as the embodiment of all that is good, true, and honorable. The Doctrine of Discovery preyed upon the human tendency towards hubris and self-evaluation, contributing to the diseased theological imagination that could not envision a world with any other expression of the fullness of humanity other than white flesh. As the European colonial Christian mind began to encounter inhabitants of the African continent, the doctrine confirmed that they were encountering a people who were inferior. This sense of superiority paired with the motif of dominance and power assumed by the European Christians resulted in a severely dysfunctional theological imagination" (88). This nuance will be expounded upon later in this book but needed to be highlighted in this moment. The narrow theological imagination found in American evangelical churches and articulated in axioms such as "the best is yet to come" is deeply rooted in a self-referential, privileged, and toxic lens of white supremacy combined with elements of hyper-capitalism and hyper-masculinity that is predominately found in North American evangelical churches.

an accessible, but not in an oversimplified axiomatic way. Thus, it requires appreciating and embracing the narrative and seasons of suffering that are synonymous with the human experience, the way of Jesus, and the ongoing exploration of what it means to be a follower of Jesus in a world of pain, sin, and loss.

Lament and the Evangelical Church

Licensed Marriage and Family Therapist, Jill Woolworth, writes in *The Waterwheel: Practical Wisdom for 64 Common Concerns*, "It's worth repeating that we cannot be anxious and grateful at the same time. Expressing gratitude for anything reboots our brains out of fight-or-flight mode. Writing five things we are grateful for in a journal or saying them out loud is comfort for our brains."[7] As a practice for engaging with anxious thoughts and tendencies, this insight and practical advice is helpful for anyone who finds themselves stuck or debilitated by anxiety. Yet, this is not lament. Lament asks an individual or community to engage directly with God with their pain, grief, suffering, or sorrow. To lament is to be a *truth-teller* of one's momentary reality or experience and so speak directly to the pain. Lament has been lost, or potentially ignored and forgotten, as a central practice of worship and formation in the North American evangelical church.

In its place, evangelical leaders have substituted lament with maxims and sayings that fail to find the beauty of lament and trust found in God when an individual or community cry out in grief. Proof texts that highlight God's redeeming power, such as those that begin with the phrase "but God" (i.e., Gen 8:1; 50:20; Ps 49:14–15; 73:26; Acts 13:29–30; 1 Cor 10:13) seek to bring hope to those who say they follow Jesus. They do so by providing pivot points that are binary and didactic in nature, helping bring new perspectives to moments, seasons, and intense periods of suffering. Despite their intentions, the practice of proof texting and providing quick answers offers a thin understanding of the power and love of God. As such, without providing thicker and more robust theological practices such as lament, the people of God on mission with God are often ill-equipped and ill-prepared to deal common experiences of death and suffering.

The North American evangelical church has stepped away from lament and sought quick, shallow responses to pain and suffering. It is important for evangelicals to be reminded of the deep, formative beauty and

---

7. Woolworth, *Waterwheel*, 23.

power that is found in lament and so embrace the liminal uncertainty that draws people to God in all seasons of life, especially suffering.

Triumphalism and Grief Cannot Coexist

When the LORD (YHWH) chose the Israelites to be the people of God, over time his chosen people who were called to be set apart mistook their chosen-ness and selection as a form of exceptionalism. After reaching the promised land and establishing the city of Jerusalem, the Israelites were already on a trajectory of hubris that caused a malfunction and distortion of their understanding of who they were in the eyes of the LORD and their subsequent role in obeying God's commands and serving those around them. The people of God repeatedly rejected the LORD (Exod 32), failed to fully disobey God's word (Exod 16), or turned their back on God (Jer 2) in a posture, practice, and pursuit of worldly power.

The North American evangelical church has exhibited similar realities, from the myth of early pilgrims moving from Europe to their own promised land, to the growth of American exceptionalism that permeates the cultural status quo, the ideology and practice of *manifest destiny* as people moved westward, and the most recent tipping point of embodied exceptionalism that moved to the forefront of the nation's imagination during the 2016 and 2020 Presidential elections. Triumphalism takes the form of unique exceptionalism where a specific people or person is believed to be more victorious and special than those around them, creating a self-perceived ecosystem that makes lament and grief incompatible with one's existential reality. Akin to Woolworth's statement above, "that we cannot be anxious and grateful at the same time. Expressing gratitude for anything reboots our brains out of fight-or-flight mode."[8] Expressing lament and engaging in the theological posture and practice of truth-telling in the face of grief and suffering rewrites the narrative and reforms the spirit and character of a person or community to such an extent that their once self-perceived reality of perpetual, ongoing victory (Rom 8:37) reorients a people and community, and so finds common ground and witness in one-another's pain.

Leading North American evangelical churches continue to espouse this prescribed, perpetual, unending form of prosperity and triumphalism that functions as a bionetwork of Christian exceptionalism equating to a

8. Woolworth, *Waterwheel*, 41.

form of Spirit-led immunity to common human experiences such as grief, suffering, and loss.

Lakewood Church, in Houston, Texas, leads with "at Lakewood, we believe your best days are still out in front of you."[9] Elevation Church, in Matthews, North Carolina states, "See what God can do through you."[10] Christ's Church of the Valley, in Phoenix, Arizona, asserts, "At CCV, our mission is to WIN people to Christ, TRAIN believers to become disciples, and SEND disciples to impact the world."[11] Life Church, in Grapevine, Texas, affirms, "Our vision for Fellowship Church is simple. We exist to Reach Up, Reach Out, and Reach In. These three are the biblical mandates of the local church."[12] While these churches clearly and sincerely seek to contribute to the building of God's church in the ecclesial moment between the now and the not yet of the Lord's return, there is a consistent and overt theme that when one is in Christ, a follower of his way, and a member of these evangelical communities they will bear the fruit of victory and exceptionalism, maximizing perpetual success, financial reward, and embodying a reality of immunity to grief and loss.

While this recognition is not affirming a theology of suffering uniquely or over and above a theology of celebration, trouble emerges when there is such an overt emphasis on victory and exceptionalism that is fundamental to the experience of following Jesus. It is almost as though evangelical churches in North America affirm an algorithm that states that once a person is (i) in Christ, (ii) seeking to obey and embody his word in all areas of life, and (iii) attends stated leading evangelical church, then they will flourish and succeed in all areas of life and become insusceptible and immune to any form of grief or suffering.

This echoes the perception of the Israelites prior to fall of Jerusalem. Mark Charles and Soong-Chan Rah write,

> Lamentations points out the faulty reasoning of exceptionalism that the traumatized remnant of Jerusalem was experiencing. As noted in *Prophetic Lament*: "The fall of Jerusalem is particularly disturbing to the residents who held a high view of their worth as a city. Jerusalem was David's city. . . Jerusalem was home to the temple of the Lord. It was the place of affirmation that Israel had a

9. "About Us," Lakewood Church.

10. "See What God."

11. "About Us," CCV.

12. "Learn about Fellowship Church."

unique covenantal relationship with YHWH." The residents of Jerusalem embraced this sense of exceptionalism and believed themselves to be impervious to YHWH's judgement and punishment.[13]

This may be why many North American evangelical churches articulate such a strong resonance with Old Testament temple language. The local church in North American evangelicalism is the locus and focus of a Jerusalem-like exceptionalism and so places with a self-perceived immunity that runs the risk of becoming theologically thin on the experience suffering and grief. Such a malfunction is immature and unbiblical and contrary to the way of Jesus, as a peacemaker, liberator, and justice-oriented presence in the world.

Grief and Lament as Habit-Forming Experiences

The year 2020 was disruptive for many, let alone the church. The western world experienced a double-pandemic that shook the foundation of many nations and caused the world to re-engage its social imagination as it grappled with the COVID-19 global pandemic, the public murder of George Floyd, and the effects of Black Lives Matter and racial justice and (re)conciliation in public spaces and places.

During the COVID-19 pandemic, the church's greatest challenge was not preaching the word of God. The local church, with the use of technology, was able to expand its potential reach of the gospel, via online services. Its greatest challenge was being a concrete, embodied presence in the world as people were unable to connect socially in-person, and in doing so speak to the grief and lament with those in their community as they witnessed the death and passing of friends and relatives to a contagious pathogen. The concrete materiality of a given community is found in the nature of the church's proximity to its community's experiences, high or low, and so know the heartbeat of its people. In *The Hip Hop Church*, Efrem Smith and Phil Jackson write, "When you don't know the struggle of a people, you don't know the people."[14] The converse can also be affirmed: when one does not know the joys of a people, one does not know the people.

13. Charles and Rah, *Unsettling Truths*, 189.
14. Smith and Jackson, *Hip Hop Church*, 92.

It is commonly agreed that the COVID-19 global pandemic increased people's level of anxiety.[15] This is in part due to their inability socially and physically connect with others. This inability and lack of concrete presence is a form of violence—a violence all people experienced during the pandemic. This violence perpetuated people's fears and substantiated their need for community. The church did not have the language to speak to grief and suffering. It could only resort to triumphalist and exceptionalism language and so embodied a thin understanding of the complexities at hand. Howard Thurman writes, "When the basis of fear is analyzed, it is clear that it arises out of the sense of isolation and helplessness in the face of the varied dimensions of violence to which the underprivileged are exposed."[16] It is true, the church community did not have the tools or language that lament offers to create space for people to engage in suffering or grief of death, violence, and racism. The cultivation of community, the practice of rituals and prayer, specific teachings of Scripture, the cultivation of common experiences and the empathy found in grieving together, and the connection associated with unity and spirituality are fundamental for people's flourishing.[17] The Barna Group affirmed, "Exactly one-quarter of practicing Christians (25%), versus 15 percent of all US adults, said they were more satisfied with their mental and emotional well-being during the COVID-19 crisis."[18] Yet, it was the absence of a church service that caused the church to go into crisis.

As the church returned to in-person services, one could not be certain that they had carried with them the lessons learned of the racial violence of the murder of George Floyd or the lessons from COVID-19. It is certain, however, that the practice and presence of the church could not only be found in a Sunday church service. The church, on mission with God, is called to preach the word and practice love and good deeds. This holistic concrete materiality or ethic[19] should be synonymous with the people of God. The double-pandemic gave churches and faith leaders the opportunity

15. Carrington et al. "COVID-19 Pandemic."

16. Thurman, *Jesus and the Disinherited*, 27.

17. More information can be found at Jacobi et al., "Associations of Changes."

18. Kinnaman, "Year Out," para. 11.

19. Dietrich Bonhoeffer, in *Ethics*, speaks of the role of the church remembering and returning to a concrete ethic that is both personal and public. Bonhoeffer's insights have influenced my understanding of the preaching the fruit it needs to produce in one's daily life with Jesus and their neighbor. I am in debt to Bonhoeffer's reimagination of the church in the twentieth and twenty-first century. Bonhoeffer, *Ethics*, 57–81.

to engage their social imaginary, aligned with the Holy Spirit, to form a new language and new habits and practices of church, specific to their community. In the early church, communities were charged to form concrete habits that aligned their thinking and doing. Lament was part of these habit-forming practices.

Alan Kreider, in *The Patient Ferment of the Early Church: The Improbable Rise of Christianity in the Roman Empire*, writes, "The early Christian apologists, in contrast, talked about habitus as well as ideas; their discourse had to do with how people live as well as what they think."[20] Kreider continues,

> Christian leaders didn't think or write about how to systematize the spread of Christianity; they were not concerned to cover the world evenly with evangelistic efforts. Instead, the Christian concentrated on developing practices that contributed to a habitus that characterized both individual Christians and Christian communities. They believed that when the habitus was healthy, the churches would grow. Their theology was unhurried—a theology of patience.[21]

A theology of patience is a community's concrete materiality. Their habits towards love, mercy, grace, and justice are found intimately and uniquely in lament. These habits, however, must be cultivated. Kreider writes, "Habitus is acquired, is learned, by incarnate pedagogies that in oblique, allusive, cunning ways work on the body and thus orient the whole person."[22] As such, the practice of this concrete materiality forms people in the way of Jesus. "They entrust all things, including their own lives and the salvation of all people, to the God who patiently is making all things new."[23] Sabbath is an example of such practices.

The double-pandemic, as highlighted earlier, offered the North American evangelical church and its faith leaders an opportunity to participate in habit and character forming practices. It would be a curious exercise to know if local communities would miss the presence of their local churches should they have closed during the pandemic.

20. Kreider, *Patient Ferment*, 94.

21. Kreider, *Patient Ferment*, 74.

22. Kreider, *Patient Ferment*, 40.

23. Kreider, *Patient Ferment*, 25.

7

Lament
Witness, but Not as We Know It

¹ O God, why have You rejected us forever? Why does Your anger smoke against the sheep of Your pasture? ² Remember Your congregation, which You have purchased of old, Which You have redeemed to be the tribe of Your inheritance; And this Mount Zion, where You have dwelt.

—Psalm 74: 1-2 (NIV)

Kathleen O'Connor in, *Lamentations and Tears of the World*, writes,

> Laments are prayers that erupt from wounds, burst out of unbearable pain, and bring it to language. Laments complain, shout, and protest. They take anger and despair before God and the community. They grieve. They argue. They find fault. Without complaint there is no lament form. Although laments appear disruptive of God's world, they are acts of fidelity. In vulnerability and honesty, they cling obstinately to God and demand for God to see, hear, and act.[1]

Laments are prayers of action and trust and petition. Prayers that call out for a witness of one's pain. Prayers that call for a witness of their people's pain. Prayers that call for a witness so that a neighbor's pain may satiate,

1. O'Connor, *Lamentations and the Tears*, 9.

44

for God to show up and do as God had promised and demonstrate God's fidelity to God's people and God's word.

Over one-third of the Psalms are laments. Either personal or communal, a prayer of lament gives witness and language to things often unseen. Mark Vroegop, in *Weep with Me: How Lament Opens a Door for Racial Reconciliation*, writes, "Lament enters the complicated space of deep disappointment and lingering hurt. [In doing so] it boldly reaffirms the trustworthiness of God."[2] Lament as a theological posture and practice calls God into the grief of the suffering people and demands God to respond. It points to the suffering of the other and asks the common question "where is God?" Lament also enquires why this event is happening. Lament also frames pain asking why God allows bad things to happen to good people. And, if God really is powerful, then one asks why does God seem to fail to show up in most desperate times of need? All these questions, fundamentally, are people bearing witness to grief and pain throughout their world and lamenting at the perceived absence of God. At its most basic level, to lament to is observe, protest, mourn, and demand God to intervene in the pain.

When the people of God fail to lament, they inadvertently separate themselves from their neighbor. Mark Card writes,

> Our failure to lament . . . cuts us off from each other. If you and I are to know one another in a deep way, we must not only share our hurts, anger, and disappointment with each other, we must also lament them together before the God who hears and is moved by our tears. Only then does our sharing become truly redemptive in character. The degree to which I am willing to enter into the suffering of another person reveals the level of my commitment and love for them. If I am not interested in your hurts, I am not really interested in you. Neither am I willing to suffer to know you nor be known by you. Jesus' example makes these truths come alive in our hearts. He is the one who suffered to know us, who then suffered for us on the cross. In all this, he revealed the *hesed* (loving kindness) of His Father."[3]

To lament is to communally bridge-build and *bridge across difference*. It is to widen one's circle of human concern and provide a language and lens, a posture and practice, a voice and heart to the injustice witnessed in the world. Be it around race or gender or economics or education, to lament

2. Vroegop, *Weep with Me*, 38.

3. Card, *Sacred Sorrow*, 29.

and witness to a neighbor's pain is to say that one is with them in this fight, just as Jesus is with us in our fight.

The evangelical church in North America needs to remember, refind, and reacquaint itself with the theology and practice of lament. In doing so, the local church will have the opportunity to reposition itself with its local community and provide a new language and new narrative with one another, not laden with exceptionalism or perpetual victory, but with empathy and grace and love.

Lament has and continues to be the elephant in the room for many North American evangelical faith communities. It must be noted that the explication of and pursuit towards a deep, formative, and true practice of lament in evangelical spaces and places is not designed with the goal of perpetuating the troublesome narrative of triumphalism that is already a fundamental concern in evangelical communities and a nuance emphasized in this paper. The explication of and pursuit towards a deep, formative, and true practice of lament in evangelical spaces and places will shift the narrative away from a success-oriented posture of Christianity, towards one that is framed in faithfulness and liminality as the people of God sit in potentially unresolved grief and with those whose sorrow and pain may never be satiated.

By present day practices and overarching pursuits, lament as a way of witness and worship is absent in many North American evangelical church communities or misunderstood as a practice that is simply seen as an addition to liturgy and practice to make the local church or movement of churches more successful. The understanding of lament is not considered liminal, nor unresolved, nor perpetually ongoing to the point that individuals and faith communities may need to remain such a posture for an unstated, prolonged period of time. Lament is a culture shifting practice that flips the script around the narrative of triumph, success-orientated evangelical Christianity. It is not merely a practice added to an equation to make the church more influential or prosperous in its local community, city, or region. But an engagement of trust and worship towards God in a culture where being a Christian and follower of Jesus might possibly mean you lose.

This chapter will define, focus, and frame lament within its theological setting. In doing so, you as the reader, will engage in an overview and exegesis of Lamentations as a way of building a thicker, more robust understanding of the nature of lament and this book in Christian thought and practice. Although not exhaustive, it is as an attempt to frame Lamentations and the practice of lament "as a resource for the work of reclaiming our humanity, for breaking through our denial, personal and social, and for teaching us compassion."[4]

As the reader, one must remember to place lament within a frame of a theopraxis of witness and draw attention to its need in this contemporary day and age. The hope is that lament will become more embedded within a social, communal, and prophetic imagination of North American evangelical communities who will recognize that grieving can be seen as the first step towards reconciliation. Lament can then help provide language to and then become an important personal and collective step towards peacemaking and bridge-building in this broken and fragmented world.[5]

If Tears Could Speak

To speak of lament as a possible first, healthy, liturgical Christian response to grief or sorrow regularly produces a reaction of discomfort or uncertainty for those who say they follow Jesus. Vroegop, in *Dark Cloud, Deep Mercy: Discovering the Grace of Lament*, writes, "In that journey [of pain and loss] we also learned that many Christians, like us, were unfamiliar—even uncomfortable—with lament."[6] He continues, "When occasionally I candidly shared a few struggles of my soul, some people reacted with visible discomfort. Others quickly moved to a desperate desire to 'find the bright side,' a quick change of the subject, an awkward silence, or even physically excusing themselves to escape the tension."[7] What story is told through an individual's or community's tears? What narrative would one see and be formed by when one hears the stories of another's wounds or scars? I hope that this next chapter will help you as the reader embrace lament as a divine liturgical practice that leads the people of God, on mission with God, to a place of faithfulness and mercy for themselves, their neighbors, and their city.

North American evangelical churches find the theology, posture, and practice of lament foreign to their cultural status quo. Moments that create existential dissonance, such as pain and sorrow, lead faith leaders to respond with relative degrees of haste and certainty that God ultimately desires prosperity, not suffering. "Unfortunately," writes Rah, "lament is often

---

4. O'Connor, *Lamentations and the Tears*, xiv

5. Katongole, *Born from Lament*, 25.

6. Vroegop, *Dark Clouds, Deep Mercy*, 18.

7. Vroegop, *Dark Clouds, Deep Mercy*, 18.

missing from the narrative of the American church."[8] Rah continues, "In the *Lutheran Book of Worship*, the Episcopalian *Book of Common Prayer*, the Catholic *Lectionary for Mass*, the *Hymnal of the United Church of Christ*, and the *United Methodist Hymnal*, the majority of the Psalms omitted from liturgical use are the laments."[9] This absence equates to a theological thinning on a number of important fronts. The role of memory and remembering is a significant and unique feature of Christian formation.

Rah outlines the imperative of the presence of lament in North American evangelical communities and its engagement with material, everyday personal and public social issues. "Lament is an act of protest as the lamenter is allowed to express indignation and even outrage about the experience of suffering. The lamenter talks back to God and ultimately petitions him for help, in the midst of pain. The one who laments can call out to God for help, and in that outcry, there is hope and even the manifestation of praise."[10]

For such a deep and instructive practice, it is perplexing that North American evangelical communities fail to appropriately engage with lament on a consistent basis. Rah unpacks this further when he frames lament within the ecosystem of sin and shame while also highlighting the overarching narratives of triumphalism, victory, and success. He affirms that the "American evangelical inability to move beyond Christian triumphalism arises from the inability to hear voices outside the dominant white male narrative. Evangelical Christians who fail to hear the crucial voice of women can easily ignore critical elements of the biblical story, revealing deep insensitivity to the reality of a suffering world."[11] Rah affirms many that North American evangelicals engage in the dominant narrative that conforms to a hyper white, male, masculine, and wealthy Christianity that effectively holds itself captive to inappropriate norms and perspectives that inhibit the role wide and inclusive expression of Christianity in its joy and praise, as well as its pain and sorrow.

Rah implores the North American evangelical church to be formed by the beauty and wonder of lament in all its pain, sorrow, and grief. Lament brings the people of God together as one understands their own narrative and story in the other. Building proximity between people and God is an involuntary biproduct of lament. Rah affirms, "Lament that

8. Rah, *Prophectic Lament*, 21

9. Rah, *Prophectic Lament*, 21.

10. Rah, *Prophectic Lament*, 4.

11. Rah, *Prophectic Lament*, 60.

recognizes the reality of brokenness allows the community to express confession in its proper context. Confession acknowledges the need for God and opens the door for God's intervention. Confession in lament relies on God's work for redemption."[12]

Lament brings together the mosaic of expression and reality in the people of God. It provides for the spectrum of humanity intentional space for the fullest expression of a collective people. Rah asserts, "Lament allows for the fullness of emotions to be expressed . . . . Suffering and celebration must continue to intersect in our communities. Diverse worship expressions arising out of a range of experiences provide the opportunity to intersect the wide range of expressions that reflect the fullness of God's shalom."[13] Shalom is a pursuit of the people of God. Thus, lament should be imperative in the lives of the people of God. Again, we must be reminded that there is an indivisible relationship in the Bible between peace (shalom) and justice. Indeed, it must be remembered that justice is a fundamental dimension of *shalom*. The Old Testament testifies that one of the things God cares most about is justice (*mishpat*), which goes hand-in-hand with righteousness (*tsedheq* or *tsedhaqah*). The two terms often appear concurrently, which only maximizes the biblical emphasis associated with both realities.

There seems to be two basic frameworks that constitute lament. The first model frames lament around four key movements; the second finds six features consistent with the practice of lament. Mark Vroegop, in *Dark Clouds, Deep Mercy: Discovering the Grace of Lament*, outlines the first model. This model can be found in most psalms of lament. Vroegop writes, "Most biblical laments follow a pattern as God takes people grieving people on a journey. This poetic odyssey usually includes four key elements: (1) an address to God, (2) a complaint, (3) a request, and (4) and expression of trust and/or praise."[14] Applying Vroegrop's framework to a Ps 77, one could observe and experience the power of lament and apply it to their own experience.

Reading Ps 77, for example, Vroegop's model begins with an address to God where the lamenter comes to God in prayer. This is, sometimes, combined with a complaint:

---

12. Rah, *Prophectic Lament*, 131.

13. Rah, *Prophectic Lament*, 136.

14. Vroegop, *Dark Clouds, Deep Mercy*, 18.

¹ I cried out to God for help;
  I cried out to God to hear me.
² When I was in distress, I sought the Lord;
  at night I stretched out untiring hands,
  and I would not be comforted.

Secondly comes the direct complaint to God. Here the lamenter identifies in direct, honest language their specific pain, grief, or injustice. There is usually an emphasis on why or how something could be happening. This can be observed in Ps 77:7–9:

⁷ Will the Lord reject forever?
  Will he never show his favor again?
⁸ Has his unfailing love vanished forever?
  Has his promise failed for all time?
⁹ Has God forgotten to be merciful?
  Has he in anger withheld his compassion?

Thirdly, one can observe a bold or brave request. It is here the lamenter is specific and calls God to act and intervene in a direct manner that is aligned to God's character and is consistent with God's promises—the lamenter's previous experience of God—and what they may have read or remembered in Scripture.

¹⁰ Then I thought, "To this I will appeal:
  the years when the Most High stretched out his right hand.
¹¹ I will remember the deeds of the Lord;
  yes, I will remember your miracles of long ago.
¹² I will consider all your works
  and meditate on all your mighty deeds."

Lastly, the lamenter chooses again to trust. One must not forget that that initial posture of lament is an inclination towards God embodied in trust, faith, justice, and conviction. To choose to trust again is one that affirms God's praiseworthiness and ability to intervene. It is to a practice of worship and formation that places the outcome in God's hands, while demanding the injustice and grief observed ceases.

¹³ Your ways, God, are holy.
  What god is as great as our God?
¹⁴ You are the God who performs miracles;
  you display your power among the peoples.
¹⁵ With your mighty arm you redeemed your people,
  the descendants of Jacob and Joseph.

Walter Brueggemann includes two additional elements to this liminal, recurring, disciplined form of anger and petition to God. Brueggemann affirms that "the classic model of Israel's speech of grief, pain, and rage has six regular elements, which may occur in all sorts of configurations. Indeed, not all elements need be employed in every such utterance."[15]

Leaning on his insights, Brueggemann outlines these six elements in the following way: (i) The lament characteristically begins by the naming of God in an intimate address; for example, "my God, God of my Fathers." (ii) the lament then moves immediately to complaint. It tells God—with some specificity—how troubled life is and what going on in the world—as if God cannot see the pain or plight of God's people. (iii) The lament then comes to its fullest focus in plea and petition. This is the point of the lament. The lament addresses God with a considerable, taxing, unapologetic imperative of action. This often includes a turn, heed, or save. (iv) In some circumstances, the complaint and petition under normal circumstance may be sufficient. The urgent lamenter does not leave their grievance at asking but says more. This is the divergent moment between Vroegop's model and Brueggemann's framework. The protest is regressive in speech, and therefore motivations are added to the petition. Such motivations seek to give God some good reasons for acting (i.e. God's virtue, their repentance, the need to set precedence, God's honor, or even God's vanity). (v) Very often the needful speaker who asks God for help or rescue from an enemy or an evildoer, does not stop at a petition for rescue. Put simply, the lamenter would like some vengeance against their enemy who has caused their hurt or pain. In Ps 54:5, the lamenter states, "Let evil recoil on those who slander me; in your faithfulness destroy them." Psalm 55:15, 23 reflects a similar reality:

> [15] Let death take my enemies by surprise;
> let them go down alive to the realm of the dead,
> for evil finds lodging among them.

> [23] But you, God, will bring down the wicked
> into the pit of decay;
> the bloodthirsty and deceitful
> will not live out half their days.
> But as for me, I trust in you.

Lastly, (vi) after their need, their hurt, their demand, and their venom are fully voiced, something unexpected happens in the psalm of lament. The

15. Brueggemann, *Psalms of Lament*, xi.

mood and tone of the psalm shifts. The lamenter's anger and protest appear to be spent, and pain—almost from nowhere—symptomatically moves to positive resolution. Psalm 35: 28 epitomizes such a conclusion, "My tongue will proclaim your righteousness, your praises all day long." Psalm 37:39–40 echoes a similar finale,

> [39] The salvation of the righteous comes from the Lord;
> he is their stronghold in time of trouble.
> [40] The Lord helps them and delivers them;
> he delivers them from the wicked and saves them,
> because they take refuge in him.

Whichever structure people adhere to, either Vroegop's model or Brueggemann's more extensive framework, the outcome has them arrive at similar points. Lament provides a focused, powerful complaint to God that asks God to show-up, be present, intervene, and restore.[16] This process of restoration is for a person, a people, a situation, or a systemic injustice.

In the Midst of Suffering

In *Dark Clouds, Deep Mercy: Discovering the Grace of Lament,* Vroegop unpacks the nuance and imperative of lament and its need in evangelical communities. Lament is framed appropriately as foundational and core practice

16. Tension exists and possibly lingers, however, when the people of God are asked to remain in a liminal, unresolved reality. To engage in the posture and practice of lament is not to add to the algorithm of evangelical triumphalism or perceived success. To engage in such a practice is to subvert the current evangelical cultural status-quo and imagine with God and in community, who he is asking the people of God to become in that specific space and place. Lament framed correctly, which Vroegop outlines succinctly in his book *Dark Clouds, Deep Mercy: Discovering the Grace of Lament,* provides a tool of agency and grace for the people to engage directly with God in their pain. Often the church has tools to engage with and give voice to success, praise, joy, and thankfulness. But what is becoming more and more evident is a curtailed equipping of the church in the absences of lament. Vroegop, reflecting personally, writes, "Through the years, I unintentionally became a lover of lament because I began to see the ways it could be practiced and the unique help it offers. I don't know many people who intentionally study lament. It is not normally explored as an academic subject. And most people do not set out to learn *to* lament or to learn *from* lament. Lament is usually a surprising personal discovery" (158). This is where the North American evangelical church should shift its practices. It is common in evangelical communities to study praise and worship, prayer, scripture, or fasting. It seems evident that studying lament would function as another equipping practice of the church, and so contribute to the formation of and expression within the people of God.

unique and fundamental to Christian theology, Christian practice, and a way of being in the world. He writes, "Lament is rooted in what we believe. It is a prayer loaded with theology. Christians affirm that the world is broken, God is powerful, and he will be faithful. Therefore, lament stands in the gap between pain and promise."[17] Vroegop continues, "Lament can be defined as a loud cry, a howl, or a passionate expression of grief. However, in the Bible lament is more than sorrow or talking about sadness. It is more than walking through the stages of grief . . . lament is a prayer in pain that leads to trust."[18] To be Christian, therefore, is to have this God-oriented tool that helps God's people, in mission with God, in the world, navigate the complexities and imperfect reality humanity exists in each and every day.

Vroegop specifically frames and defines lament. He writes, "Lament can be defined as a loud cry, a howl, or a passionate expression of grief. However, in the Bible lament is more than sorrow or talking about sadness. It is more than walking through stages of grief. Lament is a prayer in pain that leads to trust."[19] He continues, "Lament is the opposite of praise. It isn't. Instead, lament is a path to praise as we are led through our brokenness and disappointment. The space between brokenness and God's mercy is where this song is sung. Think of lament as the transition between pain and promise."[20] Vroegop highlights the liminal reality of lament that many may not appreciate. Lament is not a missing step or missing piece that evangelical communities have either forgotten or failed to engage as a fundamental aspect of their communal liturgy or personal formation. "Lament does not always lead to an immediate solution. It does not always bring a quick and timey answer. Grief is not tame. Lament is not a simplistic formula. Instead, lament is the song you sing believing that one day God will answer and restore. Lament invites us to pray through our struggle with a life that is far from perfect."[21]

Lament is not a practice that the church needs to check off or simply add to its war-chest of practices as a means of continuing their journey of taking ground or winning the city for Christ. Lament is a practice of trust and anger that subverts and challenges the dominant narrative of Christian colonization, hyper-triumphalism, and perpetual expansion. Such

17. Vroegop, *Dark Clouds, Deep Mercy*, 26.
18. Vroegop, *Dark Clouds, Deep Mercy*, 28.
19. Vroegop, *Dark Clouds, Deep Mercy*, 28.
20. Vroegop, *Dark Clouds, Deep Mercy*, 28.
21. Vroegop, *Dark Clouds, Deep Mercy*, 33.

prevailing narratives, that have been synonymous with evangelicalism in North America for some time now, no longer remain central to the Christian cultural status quo in the presence of lament.

In the midst of suffering, both immediate and existential for the people of God, lament recognizes that one does not and cannot always win. "Lament is how we bring our sorrow to God."[22] Lament also recognizes that, if the predominant narrative that an individual or community has been exposed to has been synonymous to perpetual victory in Christ but without the nuance or language of suffering as a corollary to the will of God, the evangelical church community in North American then finds it increasingly difficult to respond well to moments of pain and suffering and so provide language to these perpetual realties.

Vroegop asserts that when people lament they experience a shift or turn in their mourning or grief. It is almost as though the discipline of lament, as a way of turning in and turning towards God as a process of witness helps the individual or community traverse the complexities of grief and suffering and so call God into the work of alleviating and easing their pain. Vroegop writes,

> It is not at all clear what happens that permits such a turn. But it is clear that such a turn belongs regularly to the pattern and genre of lament. It may be that the long protest is cathartic, and enough said finally suffices. Or it may be . . . that there was in the middle of the utterance a communal, liturgical intervention of assurance that permitted a new posture of confidence, well-being, and gratitude.[23]

Lament is, therefore, a form of agency and formation in the midst of grief and suffering. Lament calls God to be present and so respond, when it seems as though God is absent, silent, and apathetic to the plight and reality of God's people's pain. Lament moves people, in God's timing, towards gratitude and confidence that was most perceived to be masked by the pain and suffering experienced by the people of God.

22. Vroegop, *Dark Clouds, Deep Mercy*, 21.
23. Vroegop, *Dark Clouds, Deep Mercy*, 116.

8

Arguing and Wrestling with God

Lament is what sustains and carries forth Christian
agency in the midst of suffering.

—Dr. Emmanuel Katangole

LAMENT IS A FORM of wrestling. Katongole, in *Born from Lament: The Theology and Politics of Hope in Africa*, writes, "In the midst of suffering, hope takes the form of arguing and wrestling with God. If we understand it as lament, such arguing and wrestling is not merely sentiment, not merely a cry of pain. It is a way of mourning, protesting to, appealing to God."[1] He continues, "Lament is what sustains and carries forth Christian agency in the midst of suffering."[2] Lament as a wrestle and struggle is what forms, sustains, and helps give language to the people of God as they engage with the experiences of grief and pain. "Without a complaint, there would be no lament. Yet . . . the practice of godly complaint [is] foreign to many Christians. This is one of the reasons why discovering lament is so needed."[3]

1. Katongole, *Born from Lament*, xvi
2. Katongole, *Born from Lament*, xvi
3. Vroegop, *Dark Clouds, Deep Mercy*, 43.

Lament is what helps the people of God engage with God's character and sovereignty in moment of despair, helplessness, and perceived isolation.

When one thinks about the wrestling with God, more often than not images or one's imagination recalls the story of Jacob grappling and struggling with God, demanding a blessing (Gen 32:1–32). The story goes that Jacob was returning from Canaan with his family, scared to death. His brother Esau was about to meet him with four hundred men. Jacob, full of fear and distress (Gen 32:7), begins praying to God in the form of a lament. Jacob begins with an intimate address: "O God of my father Abraham, God of my father Isaac" (verse 9). He moves to his petition, "Save me, I pray, from the hand of my brother Esau" (verse 11) and then quickly shifts to an expression of trust and praise in verse 12, "But you have said, 'I will surely make you prosper and will make your descendants like the sand of the sea, which cannot be counted.'" After this prayer of lament, Jacob wrestles with God until sunrise the following day.

It is during this time of wrestling with God that Jacob has his hip wrenched from its socket. As the sun rose, God asserts, "Let me go, for it is daybreak!" But Jacob responded, "I will not let you go unless you bless me" (verse 26). It is in this moment that God gives Jacob a new name, Israel. As Jacob (Israel) asks God's name, God does not respond verbally, but with blessing.

Similar to Jacob, and other biblical examples of wrestling with God in the form of lament such as Job, David (2 Sam 2:33), Jeremiah (Jer 12:1–4; 14:17–22; 20:7–18; 25:34–38; Lamentations), Hezekiah (Isa 38:10–20), and Ezekiel (Ezek 19) one goes to God and laments to petition God in the form of a grievance or cry for help from a posture of trust. To wrestle with God is to trust God for the outcome, despite the outcome. To wrestle with God is to engage directly with the one who gives breath and life and Spirit. God wants us to go to him with the full spectrum and gamut of life's experiences. He wants us to know that he can handle whatever we throw at him. The God of this world wants all of us—not just our clean, manicured, and veneered Sunday-best.

Todd J. Billings, in *Rejoicing in Lament: Wrestling with Incurable Cancer and Life in Christ*, brings this to light in the Psalms, for example, when he writes, "Writers of laments and complaints in the psalms often seek to make their 'case' against God, frequently citing God's promises in order to complain that God seems to be forgetting his promises. They throw the promises of God back at him."[4] It must be noted here that laments are not causative. If one laments, God does not act like a genie or servant, immediately fixing things. Time is not bound by the girth of the lament. If we yell louder, God does not move more expediently. This reality of time is often difficult for many to grapple with. God transcends time and so moves at his own cadence.

One laments because they trust God for their life, despite the outcome. And the timing of the response. Trust found in one's lament supersedes the lamenter's desired outcome. Billings writes, "It is precisely out of trust that God is sovereign that the psalmist repeatedly brings laments and petitions to the Lord . . . if the psalmist had already decided the verdict—that God is indeed unfaithful—they would not continue to offer their complaint."[5]

To argue and wrestle with God is to lament to God, to complain to God asking God to step into a space of pain and suffering. At the same time, it is evident that to lament is to trust God deeply. It is to trust God for the outcome, demanding God intervenes. But his intervention only happens in God's way and in God's timing.

The Silence of God

Silence can be awkward. Silence can also be sacred. The role of silence in the theology of lament functions in a distinctive and nuanced way. Silence creates spaces for the suffering to voice their grievance to God, for their grievance to be heard in its fullness, and for the recognition and understanding that *all suffering is sacred*.[6] Katongole writes, "Silence is both the

4. Billings, *Rejoicing in Lament*, 19.

5. Billings, *Rejoicing in Lament*, 58–59.

6. O'Connor, in *Lamentations and the Tears of the World*, speaking specifically about the book of Lamentations, but also alluding to the practice of lament, writes, "The one thing about which all the book's speakers agree is that God must respond to them in the suffering. God must see, pay attention, and remember them. God must take into the divine consciousness the overwhelming destitution in which they live. Only in [Lamentations] Chapter 3 does God respond, and only briefly in quoted, remembered speech of the past, not directly (Lamentations 3:57). God's voice is missing, and the book is God-abandoned. But primarily because God is silent, Lamentations expresses human experiences of abandonment with full force. And because God never speaks, the book honors voices of pain. Lamentations [like the practice of lament] is a house of sorrow because there is no speech for God" (15). O'Connor's insights bring to the fore power of and nuance in God's silence. If God were to speak, which will be explored in more detail later in this book, the suffering person or people would stop talking. God's voice would

dynamic ground within which these practices [of lament and grievance] take shape and the form through which the unsteady hope of lament is expressed in the ruins of shattered existence."[7] Natasha Sistrunk Robinson, in *Voices of Lament: Reflections on Brokenness and Hope in a World Longing for Justice*, reflects on the year of 2020. It was a year that bought two issues to forefront of north America's everyday consciousness. Firstly, the devastation of COVID-19 pandemic and, secondly, the racialized reality of violence against black and brown bodies in the public murder of George Floyd. Robinson could see that God was trying to get people's attention and recognized the common voice of women, specifically women of color, in leading the practice of lament. Robinson writes, "Whether they have been heard or not, Women of Color have learned how to cry out to God in [their] darkest moments."[8]

Robinson reflects on Jer 9:17–18 where Jeremiah shares the LORD's assertion,

> Consider now! Call for the wailing women to come;
>> send for the most skillful of them.
> [18] Let them come quickly
>> and wail over us
> till our eyes overflow with tears
>> and water streams from our eyelids.

Robinson writes, "These women were most likely professional mourners. Notice, however, that God and Jeremiah are not calling the women emotional or insignificant. The women are not silent. They are nice to have around. No, they call the women 'skilled' because the women had learned and practiced the spiritual discipline of mourning [and lamenting]."[9] Robinson continues, "They are called upon to lead the community in wailing because they had been there before! They know exactly what to do when death and destruction are all around."[10]

---

supersede their aggrieved accusations and would cause the lamenter to recoil, retreat, and stop talking. God remains silent intentionally so the lamenter can voice their sorrow. In doing so they demand—as an imperative—for God to show up and soothe their pain. God remains silent as a way of honoring suffering and the voice of those subject to injustice. It is an act of love, not an act of apathy.

7. Katongole, *Born from Lament*, 57.

8. Robinson, *Voices of Lament*, 16.

9. Robinson, *Voices of Lament*, 16–17.

10. Robinson, *Voices of Lament*, 17.

Rah, in *Prophetic Lament,* echoes this reality that is often present in the North American evangelical communities. That is, the absence of the feminine voices to lead, shape, and form a community as they grieve, mourn, and lament together. Rah writes,

> Often, the insights of women whose hearts are attuned to the heart of God are silenced because so much of our ministry endeavors arise from a culturally derived false sense of masculinity. Lamentations 1 points toward the power of the feminine voice in the biblical account. Lamentations 1 highlights the voice of suffering women as central to the experience of lament. We are forcing a theological famine upon ourselves by ignoring the voices of women. There is a deficiency in American evangelical ministry because we fail to reflect the feminine voice that is evident in portions of Scripture like Lamentations. This deficiency is to our great loss as a Christian community.[11]

What Robinson brings to the forefront of one's social imaginary[12] is a blind spot in the North American evangelical church. God intentionally creates space for people to grieve their hurt and pain without interruption. By creating space and remaining silent, God is not absent, but asks God's people to reimagine a dominant narrative in evangelical contexts. A narrative embedded within predominant culture of the church that is hyper-masculine, hyper-victorious, and hyper-hurried, unwilling to slow down and provide space for in the silence that God has intentionally cultivated for those on the margin—in most cases, if not all—who are women of color to lead the formative practice of lament.

God's silence in moments of suffering is formative and liminal. God's silence is a tool designed to equip the church towards a greater posture and practice of proximity to those on the margin. How the church responds in liminal moments of suffering, grief, and injustice, as God intentionally remains silent, is just as important as how it responds in moments of celebration, praise and joy. Rah writes, "How we respond to the possibility of God's suffering in the midst of suffering reveals our ability to engage in the

---

11. Rah, *Prophetic Lament,* 64.

12. Philosopher Charles Taylor, in *Modern Social Imaginaries,* describes the social imaginary as "the way ordinary people 'imagine' their social surroundings, and this is often not expressed in theoretical terms, it is carried in images, satires, legends etc." (23). The way people experience the world, navigate their expectations, participate in community, and make decisions, all derive from the way they imagine the world and the people around them.

depth of lament." Rah continues, "We also deal with our role as privileged celebrants when we encounter the suffering other."[13]

One can see that God's silence is deliberate. In numerous ways it opens the people of God to new, yet old, realities that have been lost in the toxicity of hyper-perpetual triumphalism. It causes people to stop, turn, and see the grief and pain of the other and so recognize the narrative of one's own journey in and through the pain in one's neighbor. Silence creates proximity between one another and people and God. O'Connor writes,

> They want something far deeper, something primal. They ask for a turning around of God, for a conversation of God's heart back to them. They want God to turn from abandoning and rejecting them. And they themselves want to return to God. They want their relationship restored. But God's turning [despite his silence] is what matters, for they have been turning to God throughout the book.[14]

Katongole echoes O'Connor's sentiment and God's matter of fact and practical approach. He writes, "God's refusal to speak has the purely pragmatic effect of creating necessary space for human speech and thus creates space for human healing."[15] God's taciturnity exposes people's pain and grief to one another; God's silence makes this inescapable. In the silence, articulating grief, pain, and sorrow requires the people of God to attend to each other's wounds and build peace together. God's silence gives all people permission to grieve, while widening the circle of human concern and providing space for the voice on the margins of society to lead, shape, and form the people of God towards a new social imaginary and prophetic reality of shalom.

13. Rah, *Prophectic Lament*, 25.

14. O'Connor, *Lamentations and the Tears*, 78.

15. Katongole, *Born from Lament*, 59.

9

Lamentations

Poetry of Loss

They yearn for God's voice, but God's voice is missing from the book

—Dr. Kathleen O'Connor

When reading the Bible, Lamentations is a difficult book for many who seek after or hope for encouragement and inspiration in their daily devotion with Scripture.[1] O'Connor writes, "For readers who live with denial, as the United States capitalist society requires, Lamentations makes difficult reading."[2] Covert despair or repressed hopelessness,[3] as Hall explains, characterizes the atmosphere of North American evangelical society. Unlike those who live on the margins of society, often described biblically as the poor, the widow, or the orphan, trauma and violence for many is hidden or

---

1. As I draw on the work of many scholars, much of my discussion of the book of Lamentations draws largely from three biblical scholars—Kathleen O'Connor, *Lamentations and the Tears of the World*, Emmanuel Katongole, *Born from Lament: The Theology and Politics of Hope in Africa*, and F. W. Dobbs-Allsopp, *Lamentations. Interpretation: A Bible Commentary for Teaching and Preaching*. The reason I find O'Connor's, Katangole's, and Dobbs-Allsopp's scholarship to be helpful is that they have all been able to provide theological commentary on Lamentations that brings technical insight into a pastoral, ministry, sociological, and theological frame.

2. O'Connor, *Lamentations and the Tears*, 4

3. Hall, "Despair in Pervasive Ailment," 91.

denied as a coping mechanism used to deal with the complexities of life. This is a survival tactic used by many, for we "humans know at a deeper level . . . that survival depends upon hope."[4]

The title of the book of Lamentations in Hebrew is *hkya* (*'ekah*), variously translated in English as "how," "alas," or "oh," which is the first word in the Hebrew text in 1:1, 2:1, and 4:1. *'Ekah* is not a word per se; it is a cry of mourning that the Israelites used during funerals and other similar occasions of grief. *'Ekah* is a cry and, therefore, represents the first and most primordial attempt to give voice to the experience of suffering and despair. This opening cry of *'ekah* signals to the reader that the book of Lamentations originally "was meant to serve the survivors of the catastrophe simply as an expression of the horror and the grief they felt"[5] during and after the destruction of Jerusalem.[6]

Poetry as truth telling, in the book of Lamentations, arose in the aftermath of the destruction of the city of Jerusalem. There is still no agreement or certainty surrounding which invasion of Jerusalem was being mourned. Ancient tradition situates this book of poetry in the sixth century BCE after the third invasion on the city by the Babylonians. The Greek translation of the Old Testament, the Septuagint, supports this contextualizing and states Jeremiah as the author. Still, some scholars challenge this dating. Yet, even if Lamentations cannot be secured unquestionably to the Babylonian period, "poetic works," O'Connor writes, "are not trapped in the historical worlds that produced them . . . [but have the ability to] take on multiple other meanings in new historical contexts."[7] The contribution of Lamentations, therefore, is a poetic gift that recognizes the common ground of trauma in the lives of God's people, while also bearing witness to the transcendent reality that all suffering is sacred.

Literal speech often fails to suffice as a legitimate tool for communication. Under the stress of pain or violence, victims are frequently left speechless without the capacity to communicate. Experiences of trauma often render people subject to such moments of catastrophe to realties of numbness and wordlessness.[8] Poetry often becomes a mode of expression that gives language to experiences that are often too deep for words as a

---

4. King, *Letter from Birmingham Jail*, 189.

5. O'Connor, *Lamentations and the Tears*, 37.

6. Katongole, *Born from Lament*, 49–50

7. O'Connor, *Lamentations and the Tears*, 6

8. Katongole, *Born from Lament*, 47.

way of uttering the ineffable. Katongole, describing the power of poetry to translate one's pain and help others empathize and bear witness to their experience writes, "When the poet or poets of Lamentations sought to give expressions to the unspeakable pain that their community was ensuring, they drew largely on the form, imagery, and metaphors of these laments."[9]

Lamentations, for those who begin in or from a place of suffering, becomes a book of solace. O'Connor affirms, "[Lamentations] serves as a witness, a knowing, a form of seeing wherein readers recognize their lives symbolically or more literally, and in that recognition, they are no longer alone in their pain. We enter a poetic space that, no matter how distant from our own lives, has strange capacities for assurance and companionship."[10] To speak poetically of one's own pain is create proximity with others, while also building agency towards God. This is the beauty of the posture and practice of lament and the complexity found in the often-ignored text of Lamentations.

A Framework of Suffering and Loss

Lamentations is written as lyric poetry within the confines and framework of the Hebrew alphabet. Each poem or chapter in Lamentations is an acrostic poem, except chapter 5, with stanzas that remain faithful to the boundaries of acrostics. Dobbs-Allsopp outlines this unique feature when he writes,

> Lamentations 1 and 2 are made up of stanzas consisting of three couplets in which only the initial word of each stanza begins with the appropriate letter of the alphabet. The first word of the stanza begins with *aleph* (the first word of the Hebrew alphabet), the first word of the second stanza begins with the next letter, *bet*, and so on, proceeding successively letter by letter through the alphabet with each new stanza, until reaching the *taw*, the last letter of the Hebrew alphabet.[11]

Chapter 3 contains sixty-six lines where each line is a verse. The poetic nature of this chapter intensifies the acrostic form of the first two chapters of Lamentations as it devotes three verses to each Hebrew letter. The first

---

9. Katongole, *Born from Lament*, 43.

10. O'Connor, *Lamentations and the Tears*, 3.

11. Dobbs-Allsopp, *Lamentations*, 17.

three verses begin with *aleph* (Lam 3:1–3), the next three verses begin with *bet* (Lam 3:4–6), and so on.

Chapter 4 does not replicate the cadence or framework of either chapters 1–3. If chapter 4 was to offer a parallel structure to chapters 1 and 2, one would witness a symmetrical frame around chapter 3 that gives credence to many interpreters' beliefs that Lam 3 is the center and climax of the book. This is not so.

Chapter 4 presents a shortened acrostic version of chapters 1 and 2 as it only contains twenty-two lines of each chapter, to make a poem of forty-four lines. Where chapter 3 intensifies the acrostic form of expressing suffering and grief, chapter 4 merely diminishes it.

Chapter 5 forsakes the acrostic form altogether. It contains twenty-two lines or verses and forms no alphabetic, acrostic arrangement. O'Connor does note, however, "Because the number of consonants in Hebrew is twenty-two, the final poem relates to the alphabet by virtue of its length."[12] O'Connor created a visual[13] that outlines the description above (see figure 1).

Although not fully evident in most English translations of the Bible, the use of acrostic poetry throughout Lamentations raises some interpretive questions. Why write within this framework of poetic form, in alphabetical order? Why does the writer use different acrostic forms and cadences and not have a similar framework in each chapter or poem? Why does the writer, in the midst of grief, trauma, and destruction, take the trouble to form and structure these laments using these various literary structures? In understanding these questions, the reader is able to be guided through the experience of trauma, grief, and devastation, both individually and communally.

12. O'Connor, *Lamentations and the Tears*, 14.

13. O'Connor, *Lamentations and the Tears*, 12.

Chapter 1	a_____	Chapter 2	a_____
Acrostic	_____	Acrostic	_____
22 verses of three	_____	22 verses of three	_____
lines each, one verse		lines each, one verse	
per letter (66 lines)	b_____	per letter (66 lines)	b_____
	_____		_____
	_____		_____
Chapter 3	a_____	**Chapter 4**	a_____
Acrostic	a_____	Acrostic	_____
66 verses of one	a_____	22 verses of two	
line each with three		lines each	
verses per letter	b_____	(44 lines)	b_____
(66 lines)	b_____		_____
	b_____		
Chapter 5			
Not an acrostic			_____
22 verses of two lines each (22 lines)			

Figure 1: Acrostic and Alphabetic Framework[14]

Katongole notes that the Jewish people read Lamentations during the annual commemoration of the destruction of Jerusalem, *Tisha B'Av*. As such, "it may be that the book was composed as a liturgical text to be recited during the commemoration."[15] Although liturgy has its place in helping readers and participants remember, a number of interpreters offer up what seem to be deeper ramifications to this complex literary structure. Dobbs-Allsopp suggests that this approach is polyvalent. He writes, "The alphabetic acrostic in Lamentations offers more than fancy window dressing for the poetry's otherwise separable semantic and propositional content . . . the acrostic, like other formal features in Lamentations has a pronounced cohering affect."[16] In the chaos and commotion of destruction witnessed by the voices in Lamentations, such structure brings a form of security that is not found in the turbulence of despair.

---

14. O'Connor, *Lamentations and the Tears*, 31.

15. Katongole, *Born from Lament*, 44.

16. Dobbs-Allsopp, *Lamentations*, 18.

O'Connor recognizes that "to write an acrostic is difficult in any language, requiring verbal fluency beyond the demands of ordinary poetry."[17] These poems are not spontaneous outpourings of emotion but carefully crafted pieces of poetic art, both individually and collectively. Functioning as an aid to memory, almost as a mnemonic tool during liturgy, the acrostics in Lamentations "expose the depth and breadth of suffering in conflicting ways."[18] No chapter in Lamentations ends in hope. Grief covers all and stifles any glimpse of optimism. The book, like grief, opens one to the reality that some pain and sorrow remain unresolved.

O'Connor and Katongole agree that the literary devices of Lamentations offer more to the reader than mere memory. O'Connor writes, "The alphabet gives both order and shape to suffering that is otherwise inherently chaotic, formless, and out of control. . . . It tried to force unspeakable pain into a container that is familiar and recognizable . . . [while implying] that suffering is infinite, for it spans the basic components of written language from beginning to end."[19] Katongole offers a nuanced insight that requires our full attention. "According to the Talmud, in the original act of creation, God used twenty-two letters of the alphabet for each of the seven days of creation. The 154 (22 x 7) verses of the book of Lamentations symbolize that even seven days of creation have found their nemesis in seven days of anti-creation."[20] What was once created, has now been destroyed.

Lamentations, written as lyric poetry within the confines and framework of the Hebrew alphabet, offers the reader a deeply formative, yet liminal and unresolved experience. Lament honors the human voice of suffering, bears witness to the chaos and shock experienced in one's own grief, and gives shape and resonance to grief that is often chaotic, amorphous, and isolating.

Four Voices

Lamentations is crafted as five short chapters or poems. These chapters not only offer the reader voices of grief and loss and protest and fury, but they also provide a cadence and framework as one engages with and processes grief. Throughout Lamentations there are four separate voices: (1) the city

17. O'Connor, *Lamentations and the Tears of the World*, 12

18. O'Connor, *Lamentations and the Tears*, 12.

19. O'Connor, *Lamentations and the Tears*, 13.

20. Katongole, *Born from Lament*, 45

of Jerusalem personified as a woman, Daughter Zion, who is left alone and abandoned on a hill (1:1); (2) a narrator who comments on the woman's situation (2:1); (3) a voice in chapter 3, who scholars describe as the captured soldier or the strong man, while others identify the voice in chapter three as Jeremiah himself (3:1); and (4) the reader leans in to the collective voice of the community (5:1). The effect and impact of these separate voices is designed to give testimony to the individual and collective experience and reality of suffering. "Testimonies are partial statements of truth, told from a limited angle, from a particular contextual space."[21] Regarding the mosaic and depth of these four testimonies or voices, O'Connor writes,

> The voices overlap and contradict each other with passionate, authoritative testimonies about the disasters they have survived. Together, they produce an oratorio of sorrows with each voice contributing a partial perspective, an intense but limited testimony about the evil that has engulfed them. The voices conflict with each other and reach no resolution. They yearn for God's voice, but God's voice is missing from the book."[22]

These four perspectives ask readers, as followers of Jesus, to respond not only to the individual encounters of grief and loss but also to the communal experience of suffering. In holding individual and collective experiences in tension, followers of Jesus are asked to engage in the complex, existential ambiguity of God's sovereignty. Lament helps one hold onto hope when YHWH (the LORD) seems silent. It also helps a community learn how remember YHWH's covenantal relationship when people experience collective loss. The way a community and individual engage in these theological complexities reveals their ability to engage in the depth of lament.

Subsequently, these four voices situated in Lamentations present various opportunities to discern their community's common ground, cultivate empathy, and reshape the character of a people hoping for God's voice in the silence. Collective lament provides the space necessary that creates brave spaces of shared belonging that must be expressed in the public arena. Brueggemann writes, "What is most needed [in one's lament] is what is most unacceptable—an articulation that redefines the situation and that makes way for new gifts about to be given. Without a public arena for the articulation of gifts that fall outside our conventional rationality, we are

---

21. O'Connor, *Lamentations and the Tears*, 14.

22. O'Connor, *Lamentations and the Tears*, 9.

fated for despair."[23] It is in this moment that one must be reminded that lament is not despair—lament is creative.

One of the unique qualities of Lamentations, in chapters 1 and 2, is the identification of the city of Jerusalem as a woman, Daughter Zion. Katongole notes,

> By depicting Jerusalem as a woman, the poetry of Lamentations sometimes focuses on Daughter Zion's female role (widow, mother, lover, and rape victim) and sometimes on her city features (walls, buildings, gates, temple, and streets). Moreover, the personification of Jerusalem as a woman not only evokes Israel's covenant relationship as Yahweh's bride, but, more specifically, results in a focus on the shame and humiliation that befalls Daughter Zion due to her infidelity.[24]

As the first and most passionate voice of resistance in the book, the female voice initially appears to be "a recalcitrant and pathetic figure."[25] Yet, as she laments courageously in the absence of comfort (1:16), she becomes a powerful literary image and rare but necessary example of a female biblical figure who speaks (1:12), resists (1:19), and empties herself (1:20) as she hungers and suffers for justice. She needs an empathetic and faithful witness to her pain—but no one will comfort her (1:21).

The second voice is the voice of the narrator who reports the disaster. At times he seems to distance himself from the described events (2:1–10); at other times he identifies with the suffering of the city and laments with her (2:11–13). There is conjecture, however, as to whether the narrator is merely a citizen of Jerusalem speaking on behalf of the city or if their voice also functions as the personification of the city of Jerusalem weeping with and in the presence of Daughter Zion.[26] Either way, each voice and each poem in Lamentations stands on its own expressing a unique perspective among the city's survivors without dominating, discrediting, or dishonoring the other's voice, experience, or perspective. The narrator throughout

---

23. Brueggemann, *Prophetic Imagination*, 63.

24. Katongole, *Born from Lament*, 43–44.

25. O'Connor, *Lamentations and the Tears*, 14.

26. In Brian Wintle's *South Asia Bible Commentary: A One Volume Commentary on the Whole Bible*, there is discussion regarding the identity of the narrator. Although scholars such as O'Connor, Katongole, and Rah identify and agree that the narrator functions as a mere observer to the grief experienced firsthand by Daughter Zion, it did seem important to offer this perspective from Northern Indian theologian Paul Swarup.

Lamentations leaves perspectives and opinions unresolved, exposed, and vulnerable, recognizing over and again that all suffering is sacred.

In the first two acrostic poems the reader is exposed to the voices of Daughter Zion and the narrator. In the third poem or chapter, the reader is asked to lean into the voice of the Geber (גֶּבֶר), the strong man (3:1; 35; 36; 39). This voice is often referred to as the voice of Jeremiah. As in the book of Jeremiah, Jeremiah becomes the chief lamenter (3:1) weeping over the plight of the city and the pain of her people. The Geber was charged with the defense of the vulnerable members of the city: women, children, and the poor. Yet, instead of protecting others, the strong man agonizingly and dishonorably (3:12–15) speaks of himself and his inability to fulfill his protective role. The strong man, the Geber, laments in captivity (3:7), imprisoned by the enemy call on the LORD to do something—but God remains silent.

Within chapter 3, the strong man's testimony of hope is brittle and obstruse. O'Connor writes of the indecisiveness of the strong man's witness, "He vacillates so often between hope and despair that his hope remains ambiguous at best. This is not to deny the presence of hope . . . but rather to question the long history of interpretation where hope washes away and silences the suffering and despair around it."[27] This is important to note. In chapter 3 some readers may be tempted to see verses 19–27 as the epicenter of this book. This would be an oversight. Chapters 4 and 5 return immediately to voices of despair, suffering, pain, and isolation. The testimony of the strong man in chapter 3 does call readers to remember *zakar* (זְכָר־), the character of YHWH in the midst of suffering (3:19–17) and how he responded to the lament (3:55–57). This is important to remember when one feels, sees, or experiences God's isolation and imperative to the practice of lament within the context of YHWH's covenant with God's people. It does not, however, silence or resolve the suffering of the strong man; it forms him and honors his pain. Rah notes that "suffering, evil and pain are not YHWH's [the LORD's] final intention. YHWH has the last word because his love is never finished."[28] It is YHWH's covenantal promise keeping character that creates space for each individual testimony to be bravely articulated. This is the formative and liminal piece of lament that speaks so intentionally to the North American evangelical church in this post-COVID and Black Lives Matter moment. It is moments like these that

---

27. O'Connor, *Lamentations and the Tears*, 14.

28. Rah, *Prophetic Lament*, 129.

give the people of God courage and despair at the same time. It was and is God's covenantal relationship with God'speople—not humanity's talent, charisma, or performance that allows the people of God to directly moan and lament.

Although chapter 3 forms the geographic center of this book of poetry, this moment of poetic hope does not conclude the book. "Instead," writes O'Connor, "the two final chapters move back to themes of grief, anger, and despair and smother hope like a blanket over a fire."[29] Its two speakers, the narrator and the people of the city, present forms of detachment and exhaustion as they describe a reality where doubt and desolation have silenced any form of hope.[30] But grief in Lamentations does not present itself as zero sum or dualistic in nature where loss can only exist in the absence of hope. Hope, and with-it God's love, response, and presence, only exists as a memory (3:55–57) while confronting people head-on, in chapters 4 and 5, with more grief and suffering.

The narrator, in chapter 4, has become a disembodied, wearied witness (4:1–16) presenting a life of fading hope and desire. The poem's second speaker is the communal voice of the people. It is their plural voice (4:17–22) that provides dramatic testimony of the invasion of the city. As a unique nuance of the book, neither the narrator nor the people demand anything from God.[31] The people are somewhat removed from the emotion of their experience.

The people continue to speak in the final poem. The people petition God in first person in chapter 5, and address God alone (5:1) that God may resolve the appeal or complaint started in the previous chapter.[32] Yet YHWH does not speak. YHWH remains silent. The petition demands YHWH's attention (5:1, 19–22) as they complain (5:2–18) about their life and context of grief in a land occupied by foreigners. Three imperative verbs dictate the opening line of the poem, declaring clearly their petition to YHWH: they want God to remember, zakar (זְכֹר); to pay attention to or

---

29. O'Connor, *Lamentations and the Tears*, 13–14.

30. O'Connor, 2002; Rah, 2015; Katongole, 2017; Wintle, 2019.

31. O'Connor, *Lamentations and the Tears*, 58–59.

32. O'Connor, in *Lamentations and the Tears*, notes in her discussion of chapter 4 and its link with chapter 5 that this may be an exegetical guess. She writes, "Because all the poems [in Lamentations] lack stage direction and linking devices, this view is no more than an interpretive hunch. What is more certain is that chapter 4 stands alone as the acrostic shortens, grows thematically thinner, emotionally less intense, and by itself, ignores God" (67–68).

look with pleasure, nābat (נָבַט); and to see, rāʾāh (רָאָה). The people of the city of Jerusalem know they are out of God's mind, out of God's sight, and distant from God's care.[33]

Lamentations finishes with an expression of the people's doubt about YHWH's care and character as God's people suffer. The poem remains unresolved and intentionally open-ended. "Just as the final words of the book of Lamentations haunt the reader and leave us to work out what ultimately happened," Paul Swarup writes, "so we need to implore our own situation, crying out [lamenting] to God . . . imploring him to restore us."[34] This unresolved reality is petrifying for the reader as wounds remain open and their reality of pain makes them ever more vulnerable. But for O'Connor, this is a wonderful space to find oneself. She surmises this needed dissonance when she writes,

> It is wonderful because it is truthful, because it does not force hope prematurely, because it expresses what many in worlds of trauma and destruction know to be true. It's very unsettledness enables the book to be a house for sorrow, neither denied nor overcome with sentimental wishes, theological escapism, or premature closure. Although Lamentations does not tell the whole story and does not contain all there is to say about God's relationship to the world, it does tell truth about the human experience of suffering.[35]

There is collective agreement that YHWH must pay attention to and remember God's people. The formative piece, the liminal space that is left unresolved, is that YHWH simply never replies—YHWH remains silent.

The Missing Voice

The common ground cultivated in the voices of all speakers is that God must, and eventually will, respond to the experience of suffering. The collective voices together desire God to pay attention, lean in, witness, and remember them. For the reader the strong man, the Geber (גֶּבֶר) (Lam 3:1), attempts to provide a flicker of hope in the middle of chapter 3 (21–27). But still YHWH remains silent. YHWH does not answer. The four voices, and the reader, wait in hope for YHWH to show, but this hope remains unresolved and

---

33. Wintle, *South Asia Bible Commentary.*

34. Wintle, *South Asia Bible Commentary,* 1030.

35. O'Connor, *Lamentations and the Tears,* 79.

unfulfilled. Such liminality recognizes lament as the central experience, in all its desperation, of deferred hope and a sick heart (Prv 13:12).

One must be aware of the nuance of YHWH's absence. Only once does God respond, but it is only in the form a quote, of indirect remembered speech of a previous moment of comfort and intimacy (Lam 3:57). Lamentations is "God abandoned"[36] where God's voice is missing, where God's presence is absent, and where God's response is deafeningly silent. This may be why readers of Lamentations find it so difficult to read. Understanding Lamentations in this way helps a reader of this text understand the sovereignty of God and the presence of God's Spirit coupled with the personal pain of loss, despair, and the unresolved silence of God. Katongole writes, "The silence of God cannot be interpreted as an indication of a God who does not care. On the contrary, the 'silence' of God reflects a deeply caring God (grounded in the covenant relationship) and may itself point to a rich theological mystery of a God who is not only moved but hurts and suffers with God's suffering people."[37]

Throughout Lamentations, the silence of God creates space for the fullest expression of abandonment. God's silence not only seeks to give honor to one's suffering but also to the human voice. If God was to reply at any moment throughout the book, the sacredness of one's suffering would be immediately undermined. For the practice of lament to be understood at its fullest, "it is a liturgical response to the reality of suffering that attempts to engage God in the context of pain and trouble."[38] The missing voice of God leaves suffering exposed so that it becomes evident and obvious to the individual and their community. "The benefit of exposed wounds is that they become visible and unavoidable . . . [and] prevents us from sliding prematurely over suffering and towards happy endings."[39]

The hidden hope of lament is that God would eventually respond to human suffering. Lament can only occur practically and liturgically without the need for response, platitude, or assurance. It is only the mystery of absence, the wrestling of silence, and liminality of the unresolved that human suffering finds its voice, honors deep loss, and so reflects vividly or remotely our own collective experiences of a silent, absent God.

---

36. O'Connor, *Lamentations and the Tears*, 15.

37. Katongole, *Born from Lament*, xviii.

38. Rah, *Prophetic Lament*, 21.

39. O'Connor. *Lamentations and the Tears of the World*, 86.

Standing in the Midst of Ruins

It should be recognized that the ability to name grief, give voice to suffering, and stand in the midst of ruins, is in itself a form of hope. Dobbs-Allsopp, in his exegetical interpretation of Lamentations, writes, "In naming grief, grief itself becomes owned, valorized, and thus ultimately consolable and healable,"[40] whether Daughter Zion utters her agony at YHWH (Lam 1:20); the unnamed narrator observes and so weeps at the grief of the city of Jerusalem (2:6); the Geber or the strong man sits in their shame, begging YHWH to not forget them (3:3); or the communal voice of the people addresses God courageously, if only with difficult questions and hopeless declarations (5:19–22). In all expressions of hopelessness, one finds movements of hope and trust.

What is voiced in Lamentations is as important to the individual and the community as the courageous practice of voicing itself. For one to stand daringly in the midst of ruins is to create brave spaces of shared belonging. Dobbs-Allsopp notes, "Lamentations both gives permission to grieve and provides vocabulary for grief. Indeed, by including expressions of grief in speech to God. Lamentations, like the Gospels' portrayal of a grieved and grieving Jesus, witnesses' grief and the work of grief as integral parts of biblical faith."[41] The poetic frame of Lamentations, therefore, teaches one how to grieve and so embodies in a holistic fashion a powerful practice of knowing that is essential to one's formation, through relationship.

Brueggemann points out that in the poetry of Lamentations, hints of hope poke through. But one should not miss the extreme reservation of the conclusion of the last poem.[42] In Lam 5:20–22, one reads:

> [20] Why do you always forget us?
> Why do you forsake us so long?
> [21] Restore us to yourself, Lord, that we may return;
> renew our days as of old
> [22] unless you have utterly rejected us
> and are angry with us beyond measure.

The last of the five poems concludes by returning to directly address YHWH. Positioned as being detached, distal, and deferred from God's people, the communal voice (verse 21) contains a short prayer of restoration that is

---

40. Dobbs-Allsopp, *Lamentations*, 37.

41. Dobbs-Allsopp, *Lamentations*, 36–37.

42. Brueggemann, *Prophetic Imagination*, 62.

seeking a revival of Judah's relationship in all its spiritual, material, and covenantal dimensions.[43] As the city lays assaulted and abandoned, raised to the ground, and defiled by the Babylonians, the people look briefly towards the future attempting to remember days gone by. Yet, verse 22 underscores YHWH's ongoing silence and rejection, adding to an unresolved, insecure, and diffident ending.

Lament, in summary, is a liturgical practice of trusting, speaking, remaining, and remembering God when everything surrounding has crumbled. Lament allows one to engage God directly and intentionally "in a complex set of practices or disciplines—[framed as] a way seeing, standing, and wrestling, or arguing with God, and thus a way of hoping in the midst of ruins."[44] Lament asks people to hold tension and engage directly with existential grief and hope remembered. Lament gives voice to and offers language about one's experience of grief, anger, and suffering. Lament seeks to remember, call to mind, or recall the covenant relationship between YHWH and God's people. Lament recognizes that all suffering is sacred and honors the human voice in the absence of God. Lament becomes the first step in the practice of shalom where, rooted in a Hebraic passion for equilibrium, all the parts cohere. It is in the practice of lament where one does not eschew or diminish the role of the other or the reality of a suffering world. Instead, lament embraces the suffering other as an instrumental aspect of well-being. Lament creates shalom; shalom requires lament.[45]

43. Dobbs-Allsopp, *Lamentations*, 148.
44. Katongole, *Born from Lament*, xvii.
45. Rah, *Prophetic Lament*, 20.

10

Witness and Memory

Anamnesis (ἀνάμνησις)—a practice of deliberate recollection,
engaged as a habit to better appreciate the intended results
of what a person or community have experienced.

LAMENT IS MORE THAN an individualistic, personal, or private practice. Lament is also a communal and people-forming practice. This may contribute to its foreign presence in many North American evangelical churches. "A plea to remember and reflect is central to lament. The vocalization of pain appeals to the conscience. It awakens the soul of the person lulled into the toleration if injustice or calloused toward those living in exile. Lament helps us hear [and see] the pain so that we can change. It is a means a prophetic witness—declaring God's truth to his people and the world."[1] Vroegop helps one understand that seeing and hearing leaders to empathy and witness. Lament, not only praise and worship, highlights the role and presence of God in God's people, thus magnifying God's power and presence in the valley of despair.

To reduce lament to only a personal or private action inhibits the conversation of communal healing and hope forming as the people of God collectively cultivate common ground around common experiences, realities, and worldview that is foundational to building a common people. Its

1. Vroegop, *Weep with Me*, 139–40.

absence combined with a reductionist approach to theology in many evangelical settings results in many swinging like a pendulum between shallow positivity and deep anguish.

Finding common ground and witnessing to one another's realities in community helps the people of God minimize such extremes. Katongole writes, "The effect is that, in the absence of a dynamic conversation about hope, public sentiments and discussions . . . tend to reflect the current political and economic moods, and thus swing between optimism and despair."[2] Understanding lament as a practice of witness, seeing, and affirming and sitting with others in their protest, builds a foundation towards reconciliation. Reconciliation is central to the mission of God and God's people as we seek to bring shalom to one another's lives. Katongole writes, "Reconciliation . . . overcomes crises, restores the dignity of individuals, and opens up the path to development and lasting peace [shalom] between peoples at every level."[3]

Prophetic Truth Telling

To lament is to be a truth-teller. It honors the depth of sorrow and pain of one's existence. As stated earlier, to be a truth-teller is a practice of agency as one speaks of their experience of grief and loss as a practice of trust and hope. It marginalizes the policing of people's pain and causes the community to sit in, empathize with, and carry one another's burdens. Such laments are found in poetry, music, or the historical and cultural expression of the spirituals. Vroegop writes,

> The spirituals help us grapple with the pain of the past. The give us the opportunity to honor the depth of sorrow—even to enter into it. Songs have a way of speaking to the heart at a level that is very helpful. Lake the psalms of lament, the spirituals have the potential to give us a new level of understanding without moving so quickly toward resolution.[4]

Spirituals provide insight into the experience and ongoing reality of many people of color in the United States of systemic racism, interpersonal racism, and historic and cultural racism. Spirituals personalize lament as a

2. Katongole, *Born from Lament*, 21.

3. Katongole, *Born from Lament*, 25.

4. Vroegop, *Weep with Me*, 59.

creative truth telling and grafts its listeners into the singer's experience. James Cone, in *The Spirituals and the Blues*, writes, "The basic idea of the spirituals is that slavery contradicts God; it is denial of God's will. To be enslaved is to be declared a *nobody*. . . . Because black people believed that they were God's children, they affirmed their *somebodiness*, refusing to recognize their servitude with divine revelation."[5] Spirituals are truth telling laments and the sound of personalized cultural lament.[6]

The power of lament in community comes when the people of God start to express their fears, sorrow, burdens, or grief. It is exposing their hidden underbelly, the things that people do not normally know or see or hear. Lament helps correct a community's practice of denial. A culture of denial where well-intentioned platitudes function as a tool of contradiction where pain or loss are perceived as incongruent with the message of the Gospel. By failing to acknowledge the potential depth of one's loss or despair, a community risks the creation of culture where narratives of victory, success, conquering, or improvement are publicly and socially permitted. This does not mean that people do not grieve. It means that people are placed in an ecosystem and environment where their pain is not collectively embraced nor is it deeply acknowledged by the community. People still go through pain. Yet, where the cultural milieu places greater emphasis on the victories and successes in life, over and above the grief and loss of life, people are then formed and coerced to *only* bring their stories of triumph, achievement, or promotion to the public square. This is a culture of denial. God has given us lament as an example of the full spectrum of life. For a community of people who follow Jesus, yet know little about the practice or importance of lament in the full life of the church inhibit the growth and equipping of the saints, in the form of discipleship, that we are all called to remember and so participate in.

Arguably, the top five most stressful life events include death of a loved one; divorce; moving house or residence; major illness or injury; and job loss. To find oneself situated in a context where the freedom to articulate these issues freely is not explicitly frowned upon but is culturally unaccepted hinders the ability for people to voice their trauma effectively and unreservedly. It is this ethos that perpetuates a culture of denial and ever so subtly champions forced happiness.

5. Cone, *Spirituals and the Blues*, 33.
6. Vroegop, *Weep with Me*, 59.

Such laments may include a miscarriage, a divorce, a cancer diagnosis, job loss, death of a close family member, or personal injury or illness. When these moments are encountered, lament is given to the people of God as a tool for processing and engaging directly with the struggle. It is God's way to have God's people engage with God directly in grief, as truth-tellers, instead of denying oneself and one's reality by failing to articulate the image of God and its associated value in all areas of life.

Lament as prophetic truth telling, as Card describes it, "represents the last refusal to let go of the God who may seem to be absent or even worse—uncaring. . . . It is supreme honesty before a God who my faith tells me I can trust."[7] At the heart of this assertion, Card argues, is that the praxis of prophetic truth telling is not really about lament, it is about our perception and reality of God. Lament helps reframe one's understanding of God's character and shows that God can truly be trusted, not only in one's moment of triumph and jubilation, but also in one's dark night of the soul, their darkest depths of despair. God wants all people to know, both intellectually and existentially that God is compassionate and loving and ever-present in all aspects of life. Lament helps people see that God's faithfulness to God's people does not change—be it in the everyday realities of one's mundane experiences or in moments of crisis and mourning. Truth-telling bears witness to difficult conversations[8] and asks the lamenter to speak boldly of their experiences of suffering, demanding that God shows up in the future, like God has done before. To be a truth-teller as one laments believes, with desperation, that God will show-up again.

Justice and Love

Katongole writes, "Biblical lament reflects a deep immersion in the covenantal relationship and with the community of faith. This observation is important because the loss of lament in our time may simply reflect the loss of a deep covenantal relationship with God and with a community of faith."[9] In no context is this more relevant than in public space and places when the people march and protest, seeking godly justice and peace in racialized moments of violent intolerance. The rise of Black Lives Matter, especially during the summer of 2020 after the death of three innocent people of color

7. Card, *Sacred Sorrow*, 30.

8. Card, *Sacred Sorrow*, 137.

9. Katongole, *Born from Lament*, 107.

(Ahmaud Arbery, Breonna Taylor, and George Floyd), brought the need for and power of lament to the theological surface of North American evangelical churches.

Cornel West is attributed to the saying justice is what love looks like in public.[10] Lament in public spaces and places takes a similar form. Lament in moments of injustice functions as the practice of protest. In doing so, the people of God seek love and justice in all areas of life, for all people. It is a reality that requires the body of Christ to contend with and for those who cannot contend for themselves. Katongole writes, "The faith activists . . . assume this ecclesiological reality. They see and understand themselves as part of this corporeal 'we' that is born in God's self-sacrificing love on the cross."[11] To protest is to lament. It is a striving to help repair the brokenness of the yet to be mended and participate in the healing of the yet to be forgiven. The practice of lament is one's first step of public, cooperative agency where the people of God, on mission with God, seek love in public as a practice of justice.

An illumination of this reality was most evident during the summer of 2020. People had had enough of the public murder of black and brown bodies. The ongoing violence perpetuated by law enforcement had become a nauseating reality of unnecessary, violent, unjust, and unloving repetition. The correct first response for many was to protest—to lament in public. To lament on the streets. To say, enough is enough.

In "The Other America," a public address given by Martin Luther King at Stanford University reinforces Katongole's affirmation. Given on April 14, 1967, King's lecture is the most poignant and effective example of his use of lament as a practice of cultivating empathy and proximity. King affirmed,

> I think America must see that riots do not develop out of thin air. Certain conditions continue to exist in our society which must be condemned as vigorously as we condemn riots. In the final analysis, a riot is the language of the unheard. And what is it that America has failed to hear? It has failed to hear that the plight of the negro pour has worsened few years; It has failed to hear that the promises of freedom and justice have not been met; It has failed to hear that large segments of white society are more concerned about tranquility and the status quo, than about justice, equality, and humanity. So, in a real sense, our nation's Summers of riots are caused by our nation's winters of delay. And as long as America

10. West, *Race Matters*, 118

11. Katongole, *Born from Lament*, 264.

postpones justice, we stand in the position of having these recurrences of violence and riots over and over again. Social justice and progress are the absolute guarantors of riot prevention.[12]

Katongole, like King, recognizes that a lament is the public language of the unheard. Katongole asserts, "What the church uniquely offers [in the form of lament], and what the lives and work of faith activists illuminate, is a theological grammar of hope."[13] Katongole affirms,

> What this means is that the church's life and work at this intersection of social brokenness and repair are not grounded in the conviction that she has something to bring, something to give to those who are suffering, but the conviction that, by standing with those who are suffering, she participates in the mystery of God's own suffering, death, and resurrection. It is this participation that mysteriously releases . . . a gentle but great force, which does not kill but renews and restores.[14]

Lament is a tool that allows the church to speak to the public injustice in the world. Lament gives voice to the marginalized and helps reorient the people of God, on mission with God to engage in the public, just, liminal, and hopeful practice that is lament.

Lament and Memory

Christian worship and practice are fundamentally framed around memory recovery, memory acknowledgement, and memory equipping. Recovery as empathy building. Acknowledgement as sympathetic proximity. Equipping as peacemaking or shalom-making. Lament as liturgy, replanted and reimagined within North American evangelical Christian practice will, once again, be properly understood as a central part of Christian formation—similar to other practices such as the Eucharist, baptism, Sabbath, and prayer, to name a few.

When writing about the modality of memory linked with the Lord's Supper, for example, both Luke (Luke 22:9) and Paul (1 Cor 11:24–25) use the word *anamnesis—ἀνάμνησις*. Defined properly, anamnesis describes a practice of deliberate recollection, engaged as a habit to better appreciate

12. King, "Other America," para. 22.

13. Katongole, *Born from Lament*, 264.

14. Katongole, *Born from Lament*, 264.

the intended results of what a person or community have experienced. It is an active, self-prompted remembrance especially as a memorial or purposeful action that catalyzes memory.[15] As the people of God experience pain and suffering and allow the overwhelming reality of their immediate condition take hold, lament—in the form of the psalms or prayer or truth telling—give language to tears and a framework of articulated, focused pain. Rah writes,

> The American church avoids lament. The power of lament is minimized and the underlying narrative of suffering that requires lament is lost. Bus absence doesn't make the heart grow fonder. Absence makes the heart forget. The absence of lament in the liturgy of the American church results in the loss of memory. We forget the necessity of lamenting over suffering and pain. We forget the reality of suffering and loss.[16]

As one laments, they begin to recall, remember, and recount as a praxis of trust to God and petition God to meet them in their needs as God has done so for many others before. Lament, as an anamnestic tool of worship, witness, and formation is used to remember the manner in which God moved in one's life retrospectively, while at the same time bringing the remembrance forward to their current moment in time. In doing so, one recalls the fingerprints of God throughout their life, petitioning God to do it again.

The practice of lament fulfils this memory building role in the life of those who say they follow Jesus. Lament helps center and remember one's identity and past experiences as they speak to the anxiety and chaos that surrounds them. Lament helps form an anamnestic posture found similarly in the distinctive practices and sacraments of baptism and Eucharist and is fundamental to a *thicker* understanding of Christ and the deep formation of God's people.

To not engage in such practices leads one to forget the goodness of God and the covenant keeping character of the one who led his people out of slavery, led them into the desert, gave them land, promised a messiah, redeemed people from their sins, is a justice-oriented God, promises ultimate victory over death, and promises restoration of a people who trust in him. He is Jehovah Jireh (the God who provides), Jehovah Rapha (the God who restores and heals), Jehovah Shalom (the Lord of Peace), Jehovah Shammah (the Lord who is there), or Emmanuel (God with us). If we fail

15. Wintle, *Asia Bible Commentary*.

16. Rah, *Prophetic Lament*, 22.

to remember that our God is a covenant keeping God, we fail over and again to embody a posture of trust towards a God who knows fully and has already experienced fully the depth and breadth and extent of pain that we may be experiencing in that moment. It is in these moments of periodic pain, when we remember, that we are encouraged to lament. Lament then functions as a tool of worship in our moments of pain.

Rah writes, "Laments are prayers of petition arising out of need."[17] Specifically, laments are complaints, requests, grievances, criticisms, groans, grumbles, moans, objections, and protests. Laments are directed at God and to God in light of an individual's or community's response to their reality of pain, marginalization, ostracism, grief, or sorrow. But laments, as one digs deeper, offer more than a mere complaint to God. Brueggemann states,

> It has been noticed by many readers of the Psalms . . . that there is a recurring, disciplined form to the complaints and laments. Israel knew how to order its grief, not only to get that grief fully uttered and delivered but also to be sure that, said in its fullness untamable, it is not turned loose with destructiveness. What we have in these poems [of lament] is not raw rage, anger, and sadness; rather what we have has already been ordered, mediated, and stylized to make the rage and hurt more effective, available, and usable. It is this ordering of raw grief that is the work of the poem and the gift of the poet.[18]

Such ordering and liturgy allowed for the individual or community, when speaking of or hearing about a lament, in public or private spaces, to say yes . . . me too.

17. Rah, *Prophetic Lament*, 21.
18. Brueggemann, *Psalms of Lament*, x–xi.

11

Lament and Peacemaking

Shalom is. . .peace with God, peace with their neighbor, peace
with the context or environment, and peace with themselves

Now WE PIVOT. In this chapter I seek to cultivate a reflective theology that
analyzes some of the predominant major narratives emanating from North
American evangelicalism that is currently present in and permeates the
cultural fabric of Hillsong California. I reflect on and seek to reimagine
how the presence of lament impacts such predominant narratives. I hope
to provide insight into and awareness of the need of lament in this ministry
context and provide a foundation for the proposed new ministry initiative.

To this point, it is necessary to reaffirm that the North American evangelical faith community needs to be liberated from and take concrete steps
toward to a new sociospiritual practice and witness. Such concrete steps,
realized within the mission of God as *peacemaking*, seeks to reorient and
reimagine the people of God towards a healthier narrative that does not include aspects of hyper-exceptionalism, triumphalism, and a perpetual pursuit of health and wealth in local spaces and spaces. Piet Zuidgeest writes,
"The church should always allow for the experience of God's absence and
religious lament at its very heart, in its care and policy, in its theological

reflection."[1] The absence of lament as an authentic practice in these settings has contributed to these contaminated narratives. Card writes,

> But there exists within American Christianity a numb denial of our need for lament. Some theologians go so far as to say these biblical laments no longer apply to us. And so, the language of confession sounds stranger and stranger to our ears. It is heard less and less in our churches, and when it is voiced, rarely are our sins genuinely lamented. Through lament we both regain a sense of awareness and a language to express the hopeless depth of sin. We discover a way to enter the Presence and there experience the despair that comes as a result of unconfessed sin. After all, can sins be sincerely confessed until their lamentable-ness is deeply felt by us and submitted to God for forgiveness through the blood of Jesus?[2]

Lament framed in this way will not be interpreted as an additional practice to a community's liturgy or formation that then improves the algorithm of their walk with Jesus. Lament, engaged appropriately and contextually, will place the people of God, on mission with God, in a liminal and formative space that intentionally slows them down and helps the community see, hear, and feel the pain of their city—in this case, San Francisco, California. Lament, in turn, will begin to be seen as a social ethic of just peacemaking, reconciliation, and *shalom*. It is this pursuit of *shalom* that one pursues peace with God, peace with their neighbor, peace with the context or environment, and peace with themselves—theologically *shalom shalom*.

Lament: Unlearning and Relearning Christian Agency

C. S. Lewis, in *A Grief Observed*, writes, "My idea of God is not a divine idea. It has to be shattered from time to time. He shatters it Himself. He is the great iconoclast. Could we not almost say that this shattering is one of the marks of His presence?" He continues, "All reality is iconoclastic."[3] Lewis, describing his personal experience with grief associated with the passing of his wife, highlights a unique and common yet rarely articulated reality regarding humanity. When people grieve, their perception of God is often shattered. People's perception of life, its moments of joy, victory, well-being,

---

1. Zuidgeest, *Absence of God*, 140.

2. Card, *Sacred Sorrow*, 21.

3. Lewis, *Grief Observed*, 66.

or success is instantaneously dislocated, disordered, and disrupted by grief. Grief is difficult to grasp and handle when one directly experiences it.

It is the presence of grief that keeps one proximal to one another and attempts to remind people of the reality of brokenness in the world. When grief is experienced, however, the absence of lament distorts reality. One needs to be reminded—more often than not—that Jesus also experienced the mystery of suffering and was not immune to its iconoclastic impact.

Jesus experiences grief or sadness at least three times in Scripture. In John 11, he arrives at the tomb of his closest friend, Lazarus, and weeps (John 11:35); in Luke 19, Jesus approaches the city of Jerusalem and wept over it (Luke 19:41); and in Heb 5, the writer affirms,

> During the days of Jesus' life on earth, he offered up prayers and petitions with fervent cries and tears to the one who could save him from death, and he was heard because of his reverent submission. Son though he was, he learned obedience from what he suffered and, once made perfect, he became the source of eternal salvation for all who obey him. (Heb 5:7–9)

Jesus' emotional laments demonstrate "the humanity of the Son of God who became flesh. They also comfort us as they point to the promise of Jesus' compassionate presence with God's children in times of grief and turmoil. [In the case of Lazarus], He wept with a bereaved family."[4]

In Luke 19:41, Jesus does not merely weep, he wails. Possibly echoing the lament of the city of Jerusalem in Lamentations, Jesus weeping over the city of Jerusalem was in anticipation of its destruction. He knew "that the city would be destroyed as a result of its blindness to its need for repentance and for forgiveness."[5] Instead of salvation, Jerusalem would experience devastation, but at this time at the hands of the Romans. Comparing Jesus' experiences in Luke and John, Katongole writes,

> The Greek word used here is klaiō (κλαίω), which may be interpreted as audible weeping and particularly "loud expression of pain and sorrow."[6] Jesus' wailing over Jerusalem is all the more

4. Wintle, *South Asia Bible Commentary*, 1422.

5. Wintle, *South Asia Bible Commentary*, 1374.

6. Katongole, in *Born from Lament*, notes, "In contrast, John uses *dakryō* (δακρύω)—a verb that is often translated into English as 'weep' and 'burst into tears'. This word is generally understood as being synonymous with klaiō (κλαίω); the only difference is the emphasis upon the noise accompanying the weeping in the case of klaio (κλαίω). This would indicate that, while here in Luke Jesus' weeping means a loud demonstrative form of weeping, a wailing, in John Jesus did not wail loudly but was deeply grieved" (146).

pronounced, not just because of the verb used, and not just because, as a man, he is doing something that women typically do, but also because his weeping stands in such stark contrast to the enthusiastic jubilation of the crowds (19:37), who recognize him as the messianic king of Old Testament promise (19:38, citing Ps.118:26). This juxtaposition—and thus the abrupt shift in Luke's account—of jubilation to lament, of (the people's) shouts of joy to (Jesus') tears makes Jesus' wailing even more striking.[7]

The direct of experience of grief wreaks havoc on people's perspectives—even that of the Son of God—but it does not need to keep them paralyzed.

Lament as a way of unlearning and relearning *agency* equips the people of God to engage directly with the grief before them. In both examples, Jesus responded to the grief before him, but firstly needed time and space to lament. Grief as an agent of disruption only paralyzes people if they fail to give enough time and space to trust, grief, and protest at and to God and so let their suffering speak. One sees that as this happens—that the sacrality of suffering is honored and recognized and witnessed—lament then becomes a mysterious creative *peacemaking ethic.* "Suffering will always have a dimension of mystery, as the Book of Job assures us, but a great deal of light is nevertheless cast by the affirmation that God suffers with humanity."[8]

Katongole writes, "The cry of lament is not simply a prayer but a social ethic—a passionate, pastoral, and practical engagement on behalf of the crucified of history. Consequently, the notion of a vulnerable/hidden/crucified God needs to play a more central role . . . than it has until now."[9] The iconoclast of grief, with the tool of lament—given to the people of God—should, in God's timing, be a catalyst of and a tool towards agency. Not in a self-help, hyper-individualistic nature. Such agency is proximal, communal, cocreative, and local. To go to God with our pain becomes the formative practice in one's journey of sanctification—the process of becoming more like Jesus, by the power of his Holy Spirit. Lament make us more mature and helps us in our journey of formation as the people of God.

People often become paralyzed by grief when they look to God as the problem or origin of pain, grief, and suffering. Fiddes reminds people that this nuance is not synonymous with lament. Fiddes writes,

---

7. Katongole, *Born from Lament*, 146.

8. Fiddes, *Creative Suffering of God*, 31.

9. Katongole, *Born from Lament*, 120.

It is true that some contemporary political theology, which affirms the suffering of God, refuses to raise the question of ultimate responsibility for evil. It is enough, it is said, to know that God suffers with us and struggles for us; it is not important to know who is responsible for suffering in theory, but all-important to know whether God is going to take responsibility here and now in practice by taking the side of the oppressed.[10]

Lament does not assert or whine to God that God is the origin of pain. Lament asks and petitions God's presence and help in the moment of grief and suffering. Lament is a petition of and for restoration. Lament appeals for God's healing hand when all seems lost.

Knowing God and Knowing Self

Deep knowledge of self and deep knowledge of God is akin to a double helix. Deep knowing of oneself comes with the ability to and opportunity of engaging with the realities of life as they are, not merely as one hopes them to be. William Blaine-Wallace, in *When Tears Sing: The Art of Lament in Christian Community*, frames the communal practice of lament as a way of truly engaging with an individual's and community's reality without the presence of spin, framing, or embellishment. Lament not only allows a people to express what is true and real, it allows a people to bring what if often untouchable into light.[11] This, Blaine-Wallace affirms, is a double-edged sword. He also asserts that "lament is an ecclesiology of the shadows"[12] meaning that lament allows what is often unspeakable to be spoken; what is often hidden, to be laid bare; and what is often suppressed, forgotten, or pushed down, to be bought to the surface of one's everyday reality.

This is probably why the North American evangelical community finds it increasingly difficult to engage with lament. Pastors and leaders are formed and framed into a *stereotype of infallibility*. When evangelical leaders face moments of leadership failure,[13] poor decision-making, or the two commonly held phrases within North American evangelical circles of *moral failure* and *fall from grace*, they are unable to participate in their own journey of reflection, because the theological and cultural status quo fails to allow

10. Fiddes, *Creative Suffering of God*, 36.

11. Blaine-Wallace, *When Tears Sing*, 121.

12. Blaine-Wallace, *When Tears Sing*, 145.

13. Graham, Ruth, "Hillsong, Once a Leader."

it. This contributes not only to the absence of lament in evangelical circles, but a fear of truly engaging with one's emotions of grief, loss, and suffering, because their theology is usurped by their own fear—a fear that recognizes a loss of community, employment, status, and power. This equates to a *double failure* of truly knowing oneself and intimately knowing God.

North American evangelical culture prizes positivity over emotional truth-telling. Tough, difficult emotions, like sadness, are not necessarily negative. They are normal. It is what makes us all human. At the heart of lament is a recognition that a failure to acknowledge difficult emotions through forced, false positivity is a failure to know, see, and love ourselves—and to know, love, and trust God. It is an unseeing of ourselves and a blindness towards God.

The practice of lament helps contribute remedy this double failure. Bessel van der Kolk, in *The Body Keeps the Score: Brain, Mind, and Body in the Healing of Trauma*, writes, "The greatest source of suffering comes from the lies we tell ourselves . . . one is urged to be honest with themselves about every aspect of their experience. People can never get better without knowing what they know and feeling what they feel."[14] Echoing this assertion, O'Connor writes, "Lamentations calls us to a conversion of ourselves toward ourselves so that we can turn to God and others. It invites a seeing of the anxiety, despair, and the apathy that prevent us from knowing our connections with others."[15] Brené Brown speaks of courage and vulnerability as two keys to unlock such knowledge. She writes,

> What most of us fail to understand . . . is that vulnerability is also the cradle of the emotions and experiences that we crave. Vulnerability is the birthplace of love, joy, courage, empathy, and creativity. It is the source of hope, empathy, accountability, and authenticity. If we want greater clarity in our purpose or deeper and more meaningful lives, vulnerability is the path."[16]

For a person or people to know themselves deeply and to know God intimately, lament is the path. Lament engages one vulnerably and then, vulnerably engages God. It is also the path towards peace with ourselves, our context, our neighbor, and with God. Shalom making begins with the process of reconciliation and peacemaking of ourselves as an intentional step towards the avowal of our reality.

14. Van der Kolk. *Body Keeps the Score*, 25–26.

15. O'Connor, *Lamentations and the Tears*, 108.

16. Brown, *Daring Greatly*, 34.

To unlearn the old narrative and relearn this new narrative takes time and reflection. Jesus often gave himself time to reflect, process, pray, and seek a deeper knowledge of God and deeper knowledge of himself (Matt 14:1–13; Mark 6:30–32; Luke 5:16; 6:12–13; 22:39–44). He would use time to seek and discern God's will, as well as lament in moments of grief and anticipated pain. It is here that Jesus teaches the people of God a key lesson: no one learns from experience alone. People only learn from the experiences they reflect upon, pray about, and then articulate. "Because if the church is to participate in the life and the activities of God, we believe our work is to discern ways we are to actively enter into God's initiatives in the world. What is God doing in us and around us? What does God want to do? The purpose of theological reflection is to help us be wiser and more faithful in our discernment and participation,"[17] and deep, intimate knowledge of God and self. "To have an intimate partnership with someone is to expose ourselves to risk."[18] Ultimately, mutual vulnerability in the practice of lament becomes a source of strength. It leads to a deep and intimate knowledge of God and oneself, in community.

Pain and Proximity

Lament is not anti-joy or anti-happiness. What makes lament revolutionary within the North American evangelical church context, is that lament is anti-forced happiness. Shelby Forsyth, writes, "We often stop ourselves from feeling our grief because we're afraid to feel. But we also stop ourselves from feeling our grief because we think no one else wants to see it."[19] As a consequence, one tends to push grief down to a place in their mind or spirit that is difficult to access. As this happens, people tend to become less accessible and more distal in their relationships.

This speaks to an aspect of North American evangelical theology that is prevalent in my local city, San Francisco. To speak of one's relationship to or interaction with or salvation in Christ is to speak of one's individual identity in isolation to their community. Joys, victories, and successes are common narratives within my local evangelical frame. In a socioeconomic context like San Francisco, where the median cost of housing is the

17. Branson and Martinez, *Churches, Cultures, and Leadership*, 44.

18. Waldinger and Shulz, *Good Life*, 183.

19. Forsythia, *Permission to Grieve*, 83.

highest in the nation,[20] theological framing is often founded around financial wealth, employment, promotion, or healing. Such predominant narratives skew one's perception of walking with Christ as ongoing, perpetual, victorious Christianity. This narrative has marginalized the church from the city at large, its issues of homeless, affordable housing, and drug use.

The practice of lament challenges this ongoing narrative and asks the people of God who call San Francisco home to invert their theological narrative. To lament cultivates common ground. Speaking of his experience with racism in his community during the height of the Black Lives Matter movement in 2020, Vroegop asserts that his lament of racial violence as a privileged, white male helped him bridge-build with those in his local community. "Lament opened a door for us to walk together."[21]

To lament one's pain and grief also inverts the narrative of objectifying people in large church communities due to a lack of proximity or relationship. Christopher James, in *Church Planting in Post-Christian Soil: Theology and Practice*, stresses the need to approach neighbor [and those in our community] as subject rather than object.[22] He asserts that many evangelical church communities "fail to reverently attend to persons and unique communities to which God has called them. Not only is this approach strategically unwise, it is dehumanizing because it treats others as objects, as holes that need to be filled, rather than as subjects and actors with their own God-given agency."[23] To share pain vulnerably as lament is to bring people closer together. Similar to laughter, lament widens one's circle of human concern. Ann Weems writes, "Lamenting and laughter sit side by side in a heart that yearns for the peace that surpasses understanding."[24]

Lament is not defined to be confined to the church. It is a tool of and for peacemaking in all areas of life. Allender writes, "Lament opens the heart to wrestle with a God who knows that sorrow leads to comfort and lament moves to praise, as sure as the crucifixion gave way to resurrection. There should be no question that God does not want us to sing lament as the staple of our worship, nor should it be our internal hymn of choice. Lament is not an end in itself."[25] Lament builds proximity among the people of God as they share bravely their protest to God in the presence of others.

20. Bowles, "How San Francisco Became."
21. Vroegop, *Weep with Me*, 74.
22. James, *Church Planting*, 149.
23. James, *Church Planting*, 149.
24. Weems, *Psalms of Lament*, xxi.
25. Allender, "Hidden Hope in Lament," para. 72.

This narrative of vulnerability, via lament, is a difficult narrative for any evangelical church. It asks the evangelical community in North America to recognize that everything is not alright, and the way the church attempts to theologically frame the world through stated narratives that are only full of victory, exceptionalism, and triumph, lament affirms that it is not meant to be that way. Rebekka A. Klein, describing the phenomenology of lament in *Evoking Lament: A Theological Discussion*, writes, "To lament implies, therefore, to search for new orienting clues allowing a proper response to what happened without denying its demand . . . . Theology has not to ask whether the lamenter is justified, but how the facticity of suffering from evil, death or harm can be reoriented in lament and in the horizon of faith."[26] Such orientation is both upward and outward: towards God and between one another. Lament thus becomes a community building and community fortifying practice of trust, hope, and solidarity.

Public Justice and Communal Hope

The reign of God or the kingdom of God is not a place. It is a process and a practice of peacemaking and public justice in all areas of life. Glen H. Stassen, a former personal mentor and professor emeritus, before his passing affirmed that the *kingdom of God* is "a process of peace, justice, and the reign of God. In our language, a better translation is *God's reigning* or *God's delivering* than God's Kingdom."[27] When the North American evangelical church speaks of the kingdom, it is done so with a frame toward and reflection of Old Testament temple theology. Kingdom principles or kingdom culture is a way of stating or manipulating the people of God toward mundane measurements of perceived success. These come in the form of Sunday church attendance; tithing or giving; church growth; and narratives of financial growth, to name a few. God's reign, as Stassen affirms, does not state a frame of principles, but a frame of practices. "The most effective way to drain a principle of its power," he writes, "is not to deny the principle but to affirm it in general while refusing to discuss the specifics."[28] A principle with specifics becomes a practice.

---

26. Eva Harasta and Brian Brock (eds). *Evoking Lament: A Theological Discussion.* (New York, NY: T&T Clark International, 2009), 22.

27. Glen H. Stassen. *Just Peacemaking: Tranformative Initiatives for Justice and Peace.* (Louisville, KY: Westminster John Knox Press, 1992), 41.

28. Ibid., 55.

The pursuit and theology of lament is not a principle in itself. It is a practice and way of being in the world. Lament in the contexts and imperatives of public justice and communal hope demonstrate a people's spiritually mature response to sadness, violence, and grief. A church community's spiritual aliveness is found in its ability to bring these public injustices to God, a lament, in hope that God will show up and intervene, bringing justice to an unjust world.

Justice and hope are not isolated pursuits. Within the frame of peacemaking and reconciliation, lament acts as a way of being in the world that calls the people of God together horizontally and asks God to vertically intervene. Lament is a dynamic practice of public truth-telling that seeks reconciliation and peacemaking in public spaces and places. Emmanuel Katongole and Chris Rice, in *Reconciling All Things: A Christian Vision for Justice, Peace, and Healing*, write about the imperative of reimagining the posture and practice of the church. They write,

> Another way of misreading the story is to see reconciliation as solely a vertical movement, restoring people to God. That restoration is certainly at the heart of the story and its good news. But what is also clear from this story is that many other gifts flow from God's gift of reconciliation, including a special commission. Paul continues, "We are therefore Christ's ambassadors, as though God were making his appeal through us. We implore you on Christ's behalf: be reconciled to God" (2 Corinthians 5:20). Within the reality of "reconciling the world to himself in Christ" (2 Corinthians 5:19), God's gift of reconciliation disrupts neat distinctions between vertical and horizontal. The story is both the interior and the exterior, contemplation and action, sanctuary and streets, heart and body, worship and activism, theory and practice, desires, and deeds, preaching and living, individual and community, baptism and politics, praying and prophesying, church and world. God's mission of reconciliation challenges, moves beyond, even explodes these conventional distinctions.[29]

This dynamic approach is a fundamental piece found in the practice of lament and when engaged well would help the North American evangelical church participate thickly and deeply in a robust practice of reconciliation and peacemaking, especially at the intersection of race, racial bias, and racial violence.

29. Katongole and Rice, *Reconciling All Things*, 44.

No Justice, No Peace

Considering a theology and practice of lament as practice of peacemaking, one cannot help but be mystified by the public practices of the North American evangelical community in recent years. During the 2016 Presidential election, over 80 percent of white evangelicals voted for Donald Trump to be the forty-fifth president of the United States. Despite the pushback since the 2016 election, not much changed in 2020. "Exit polls showed that 75% of white evangelicals voted for Trump [in 2020], compared with 81% four years ago. The group, which makes up almost one in five of the US electorate, carries significant weight and was credited with being a major factor in Trump's 2016 victory."[30] The impact of this reality was jarring and disruptive for many followers of Jesus and evidence that North American evangelicals had an inappropriate relationship with issues pertaining to public, communal justice.

The North American evangelical church exists within a cultural frame that has reduced its diverse expression, voice, and mosaic. Where this cultural frame has malfunctioned even further one finds a cultural blind spot of racism, sexism, and cultural marginality. A captivity such as this manifests toxic realities of white supremacy, misogyny, and sexism that are alien to the expression and mission of God. Rah writes,

> The phrase captivity of the church points to the danger of the church being defined by an influence other than the Scriptures. The church remains the church, but we more accurately reflect the culture around us than the characteristics of the bride of Christ. We are held captive to the culture that surrounds us. To speak of the white captivity of the church is an acknowledgement that white culture has dominated, shaped, and captured Christianity in the United States. At times, the white evangelical church has been enmeshed with Western, white American culture to the great detriment of the spread of the gospel.[31]

A city like San Francisco is a mosaic of expression, cultural practices, communal beliefs, and polyvalent ideas. It was once described and still defines itself as the Paris of the West. Yet, local evangelical communities in San Francisco have been unable to replicate or mirror the cultural diversity and expression of the city. Despite the church's leadership crisis, failures, and

---

30. Sherwood, "White Evangelical Christians," para. 2.

31. Rah, *Next Evangelicalism*, 21–22.

repeatedly reported internal cultural concerns,[32] local evangelical churches has mirrored the white cultural captivity of the church where a white male culture have dominated, shaped, and captured the Christian expression of this community at large. This was why the church found it so difficult to speak to, affirm, or participate in marches and riots specific to the repeated murder of black and brown bodies during the summer of 2020. May evangelical leaders seemed to find it difficult to graft themselves into and create a thicker theology around the loss and grief associated with the COVID-19 pandemic. These church leaders could not speak well to either of these moments of public grief, trauma, and loss.

In moments of injustice, forced positivity is a form of denial. It is cruel, unkind, and ultimately ineffective. It has the propensity to perpetuate trauma and does not have the healing impact it may intend. Charles and Rah write,

> Traumatized people often cling to a false sense of security. The trauma of white America emerged from embracing dysfunctional power that oppressed others. Out of that trauma, white America continues to cling to a false sense of security. Despite the power of the gospel that attests to a divergent narrative, white American evangelicals and white liberal Christians have embraced narratives of exceptionalism and triumphalism. These dysfunctional narratives embraced by a traumatized people are amplified by a hyper-individualism that serves as a blinder to the reality of corporate sin and corporate trauma.[33]

This is why the narrative of lament is imperative to the formation of this community and helps invert these flawed narratives that permeate North American evangelical communities. Lament would help equip local, faithful communities in San Francisco with a tool of worship and trust that would help them engage directly with and speak to these public, unjust narratives that trigger and cause personal and collective trauma.

---

32. Hillsong has been in the news for well over three years now. News and media outlets have documented thoroughly many aspects of the church's leadership crisis, closing of church campuses, and shrinking numbers. While this is not the focus of this book, it must be acknowledged. This reality also speaks to the need for a theology of lament to permeate the community over time and so change the narrative from one of a white, male dominated cultural captivity, to a diverse expression of Christianity cultivated from the margins of society, that is faithful to the call of Jesus to be shalom-makers and reconcilers in his name.

33. Charles and Rah, *Unsettling Truths*, 188.

To articulate the phrase—no justice, no peace—is to lament. It is a recognition of the trauma and violence that has occurred, and God seems to remain absent. When it was shouted across America during the summer of 2020, it was often led by young, queer, people of color. Those that were least impacted by the racialized violence against black and brown bodies at the hands of law enforcement were not the first to fill the streets.

Nicholas Wolterstorff, in *Justice: Right and Wrongs*, writes "God desires that each and every human being shall flourish . . . and experience what the Old Testament writers call shalom. Injustice is perforce the impairment of shalom. That is why God loves justice. God desires the flourishing of each and every one of God's human creatures; justice is indispensable to that. Love and justice are not pitted against each other but are intertwined."[34] To comprehend the gospel from below and cultivate a theology and practice of lament that is not emblematic to a white Christian expression of Christ, it is imperative that the people of God embrace liminality and abdicate their desire for a power that manipulates the wider population. This is not merely a spiritual affirmation. It is a concrete, social, economic, and holistic pursuit that is fundamental to the gospel and linked intimately to the well-being of the poor, the widow, and the orphan of society.

The evangelical church in the United States (and the West) finds this work difficult. The evangelical community has a disproportionate affinity with power, wealth, and prosperity. This theology does not witness the work of gospel from below but embodies a form of triumphant Christianity that perpetuates the status quo of power and blessing towards those who already possess it. Desmond Tutu affirmed, "If you are neutral in situations of injustice, you have chosen the side of the oppressor. If an elephant has its foot on the tail of a mouse, and you say that you are neutral, the mouse will not appreciate your neutrality."[35]

Cheap Hope

As stated earlier, lament is anti-forced happiness. Lament allows the people of God, on mission with God, to become as acquainted with the depth of pain and sorrow, without being overwhelmed, as one is with the ecstasy of joy and wonder, without being overawed. This is an important nuance for those who call San Francisco home. The cool grey city of love is majestic

34. Wolterstorff, *Justice*, 82.
35. Brown. *Unexpected News*, 39.

in its natural beauty and ma-nmade wonders. The city of hills adjacent to the Golden Gate, the entrance to San Francisco Bay, with its crown—the Golden Gate Bridge—is captivating to locals and tourists alike. Juxtaposed to this beauty is the city's underbelly of rampant crime, homelessness, and growing fentanyl crisis.[36]

To navigate this city theologically, as God calls God's people to do, one cannot remain enamored with either of these contrasting narratives or realities. The posture and practice of lament helps one remain deeply hopeful, despite the possible paralyzing realities of the city. Vroegop asserts, "Practicing lament in the more common frustrations and less severe sorrows not only brings comfort but also develops a fluency in the language of loss."[37]

One of the overarching narratives of North American evangelicalism is the shallow belief that in moments of pain and sorrow one must believe for the best and so speak it into life. This word of faith theology, although well-intended, crafts a landscape that is inhospitable to the engagement and articulation of defeat, lament, sorrow, or loss. When a community of people or an individual comes face-to-face with a moment of grief or even disappointment, the practice of lament is void in this hyper-positive reality. Without lament, one does not have the tools to engage in the practice of reconciliation with themselves, their neighbor, or their community. This may be why, for example, when people become offended at an individual in their church community, they find it difficult to reconcile their offence, pain, or sorrow. Such sorrow manifests itself quickly into pain, and people then become offended at the church—the absence of lament created a narrative and lens that moves turns a personal relationship, that is subjective, into an objective, disassociated reality. This is why Katongole and Rice's assertion is so poignant: "Reconciliation without lament cheapens hope."[38]

Lament, within this cultural ecosystem of false-positivity, cheap hope, and sanitized grief inhibits the people of God from engaging well with themselves, their neighbor, their context, and with God—the four-fold movement of peacemaking or more correctly articulated, shalom making. Forsyth writes, "Grief does not want to be held, blocked, or braced against. Grief does not want to be quarantined, scrutinized, or shamed into

---

36. Walker, "San Francisco Seeks More Ideas."

37. Vroegop, *Dark Clouds, Deep Mercy*, 163.

38. Katongole and Rice, *Reconciling All Things*, 88.

disappearing. Just like every other emotion, grief wants to be able to move through you, free from judgement, criticism, or camouflage."[39]

Dietrich Bonhoeffer, in *The Cost of Discipleship*, speaks in great detail about cheap and costly grace. Writing critically about the thin state of the church, Bonhoeffer asserts, "Cheap grace means grace as a doctrine, a principle, a system. . . . An intellectual assent to that idea is held to be of itself sufficient to secure remission of sins."[40] Bonhoeffer continues, "Cheap grace means the justification of sin without the justification of the sinner. . . . Cheap grace is the preaching of forgiveness without requiring repentance, baptism, without church discipline, Communion without confession, absolution without personal confession. Cheap grace is grace without discipleship, grace without the cross, grace without Jesus Christ, living and incarnate."[41]

Bonhoeffer understood the imperative of a divergent posture and practice of living that costs a disciple, of the way of Jesus, their way of life as they know it. Too often, the narrative North American evangelicalism is one that is not too disparate from the way, movement, and practices of life of one's neighbor who does not know Christ or call themselves a follower of Christ.

Bonhoeffer also inferred that individual and communal identity can only be formed in concrete materiality—another way of saying that costly practices aligned to the way of Christ. He was insistent on doing away with rhetoric assumptions of the world and instead encouraging the people of God to explore creatively how Christ was manifest in one's everyday way of life. It is through the posture and practice of lament that one moves from cheap hope to costly hope. In contexts of racism, violence, gender, economic, or social upheaval, that the people of God are called to participate in the practices of lament that help lead the people of God towards transforming initiatives[42] that mend, heal, and liberate. This is imperative to the people of God and fundamental to the work of the church.

---

39. Forsythia, *Permission to Grieve*, 80.

40. Bonhoeffer, *Cost of Discipleship*, 43.

41. Bonhoeffer, *Cost of Discipleship*, 44–45.

42. Glen Stassen's Just Peacemaking paradigm speaks extensively of Jesus' transforming initiatives in his Sermon on the Mount. In *Just Peacemaking: Transforming Initiative for Justice and Peace*, Stassen writes, "It is striking how many of the transforming initiatives in the Sermon on the Mount are steps in peacemaking. Go talk to your brother or sister and seek to be reconciled; go two miles; give to the one who begs; love your enemies; pray for them; seek first God's reign and justice; judge not but forgive and take

The narrative of cheap hope is not merely a function confined to the four walls of the church, but one that must be evidenced and practiced in all areas of life—especially with those who suffer in this city. To suffer with someone as they participate in their journey of lament is to engage in a deep hope and deep trust that God will remember them and not forsake them. To lament with others is to engage in the narrative of deep reconciliation and shalom-making.

As such, this is where the narrative diverges from many mainline evangelical church communities in North America; to form a deep hope, one acknowledges intellectually, theologically, and existentially that suffering is fundamental to the transformation and renovation of a life in Christ. The theology of lament acknowledges that there can be no liberation, no transformation without suffering.

Bonhoeffer was aware of this. Martin Luther King, in his very public journey in civil rights, was aware of this. James Cone, in *The Scandal of a Crucified World: Perspectives on the Cross and Suffering*, writes, "As a Christian whose faith was derived from the cross of Jesus, Martin King believed that there could be no true liberation without suffering. Through nonviolent suffering, he contended, blacks would not only liberate themselves from the necessity of bitterness and feeling of inferiority towards whites but would also prick the conscience of whites and liberate them from a feeling of superiority."[43]

To form a deep hope, one must understand the profound formation that occurs in the liminal space between the *now and not yet*. It is an eschatological reality that is imperative for a reimagined narrative that reforms the posture and practice of the local church in San Francisco. This reimagined formation slowly shifts the focus of the church from hyper-triumphalism to common suffering; from hyper-individualism to communal expression; from perpetual victory to the language of lament; from *the best is yet to come* to *yes, I see your grief and recognize that all suffering is sacred.*

the log out of your own eye. Sometimes these steps are seen merely as illustrations of a general theme such as love your enemy. I [Stassen] want to suggest that we take them as concrete steps, each to be taken seriously. . . . Though the apostle Paul did not point to Jesus' teachings as authoritative, he seldom mentioned any of Jesus' specific teachings. It is striking then, that most of the few references Paul does make to Jesus' teachings are about peacemaking. This emphasis hints at how central he understood peacemaking to be for the gospel of Jesus Christ and the mission of the church" (53, 55). It is these transformative initiatives that are fundamental example of concrete practices, like lament, that contribute to the inversion of the narrative of evangelicalism in north America.

43. Tesfai, *Scandal of a Crucified World*, 52.

Lament moves a people towards one another as we see our own story of grief in our neighbor's expression of sorrow, as we remember the way God eventually showed up in God's timing. Katongole and Rice write,

> The problem with individualistic Christianity is what we call "reconciliation without memory," and approach that ignores the wounds of the world and proclaims peace where there is no peace. This shallow kind of Christianity does not take local places and their history of trauma, division, and oppression seriously. It abandons the past too quickly and confidently in search of a new future. Reconciliation as evacuation detaches the gospel from social realities and leaves that messy world to social agencies and governments. The result is a dualistic theology and superficial discipleship that separates individual salvation from social transformation.[44]

Deep hope and *shalom-making* cannot detach salvation from social transformation. Lament helps the people of God recognize their role in one another's lives and so contribute to the posture and practice of peacemaking in local spaces and places, like San Francisco.

Lament and Shalom

In a National Public Radio interview toward the tail end of the COVID-19 pandemic, clinical psychologist Mary-Frances O'Connor asserted that, although the realization of grief and loss is hard to face, one should not avoid them or attempt to hide from them as a strategy toward healing and finding peace. O'Connor is an associate professor of psychology at the University of Arizona and studies what happens in someone's brain when they experience grief. O'Connor asserts that when people first encounter grief, they attempt to find new habits to engage with and deal with the sudden shock, loss, or sorrow. She states, "What we see in science is, if you have a grief experience and you have support so that you have a little bit of time to learn, and confidence from the people around you, that you will in fact adapt."[45]

The pursuit of new habits is the pursuit of new practices that cultivate the whole person and returns the brain and the body not only to equilibrium but towards a reality of human flourishing and shalom. Too often, the narrative within evangelical settings is to pursue experiences that feed the

44. Katongole and Rice, *Reconciling All Things*, 28.
45. McCoy, Berly, "How Your Brain Copes," para. 4.

individual's soul or heart. This may include going on vacation, eating well, or exercising. Other practices help the individual escape the reality of their grief for a moment. These practices may not be as healthy and may lead to addiction or further grief and sorrow. Some people in their moments of grief may turn to alcohol or harder, illicit drug use. The National Library of Medicine published the results of a survey from 2012 titled "Alcohol Use in the First Three Years of Bereavement: A National Representative Survey." The report affirmed, "The rate of men clinically at-risk concerning alcohol consumption among the non-bereaved is 12.9%, and among men bereaved for one year is 18.4%, while 29.8% among men bereaved for two years."[46] This rate is alarming and speaks to the need of other habit-forming practices that help the church deal directly with grief.

A more healthy and direct response is needed in moments of grief and sorrow. Lament is the tool that achieves such a response. Berly McCoy, in "How Your Brain Copes with Grief and Why it Takes Time to Heal," echoes this sentiment. She writes,

> I think when you care for someone who is going through this terrible process of losing someone, it really is more about listening to them and seeing where they're at in their learning than it is about trying to make them feel better. The point is not to cheer them up. The point is to be with them and let them know that you will be with them and that you can imagine a future for them where they're not constantly being knocked over by the waves of grief.[47]

McCoy does not affirm any form of platitudes. She rejects them. The evangelical response in moments of grief may include (1) the best is yet to come, (2) everything happens for a reason, (3) this is all part of God's plan, (4) don't worry, God is in control, (5) God will work this out for your good, or (6) God's ways are not our ways. These responses do not offer any help, provide any space to grieve, or recognize the sacrality of suffering. This is why lament is imperative to the narrative, theology, shalom-seeking practices of evangelical communities. "Lament is not a path to worship, but a path of worship."[48] Lament is a healthy direct way of engaging with one's grief, sorrow, or pain.

Walter Brueggemann, in *Peace*, critiques the movement of shalom within the context of the North American church and the inappropriate,

---

46. Pilling et al., "Alcohol Use," para. 3.

47. McCoy, "How Your Brain Copes," para. 17.

48. Card, *Sacred Sorrow*, 21.

uncommon flow of peace-giving practices from the wealthy and rich to the underresourced and underprivileged. Essentially, if the holistic peace that God offers in the form shalom, is not a common peace accessible to all and for all people, then it is no peace at all. An articulated peace without lament is, pragmatically, not the shalom that God is talking about. Woven within the fabric of a hyper-individualized and locally detached peace one finds lament absent from the witness and worship of the people of God. Brueggemann writes,

> Shalom in a special way is the task and burden of the well-off and powerful. They are the ones held accountable for *shalom*. The prophets consistently criticized and polemicized against those well-off and powerful ones who legitimized their selfish prosperity and deceived themselves into thinking it was permanent. The prophetic vision of shalom stands against all private arrangements, all "separate peaces," all ghettos that pretend the others are not there. Religious legitimacy in the service of self-deceiving well-being is a form of chaos. *Shalom* is never the private property of the few.[49]

To pursue the shalom of God is to do so concretely. To lament is not an intellectual assent, it is an existential, engaging, public and personal, memory-inducing, people-forming practice. Lament is the embodiment of vulnerability. Katongole affirms this when he writes, "God is not inviting us simply to affirm as list of abstract beliefs but rather to set out on an adventure. If the journey calls for great skillfulness and discipline, the most vital skill required is memory."[50] Lament helps one recall, retain, recollect, and not forget the presence of God in their moments of pain.

To lament is counter cultural. The posture and practice of lament recognizes that God is still with us, despite what one may be going through. It is the entry point towards healing that must engage directly in the fullness of its reality so one does not forget the eventual healing hand of God. Rah asserts, "The blind spots caused by swimming too deeply in society's cultural values may be remedied by offering a radically different set of practices that gesture toward a new reality. Combating injustice may require not only the setting aside of materialistic practices, but the participation in a new set of practices. These new practices must include the practice of lament."[51]

---

49. Brueggemann, *Peace*, 19–20.

50. Katongole and Rice, *Reconciling All Things*, 49.

51. Rah, *Prophetic Lament*, 154.

12

Lament, Liminality, and Evangelical Triumphalism in America?

Learning to attend to the city's wounds...

Prior to the COVID-19 pandemic, in January 2020, Hillsong San Francisco would have its Sunday services at August Hall in downtown San Francisco, one block from Union Square. Each and every Sunday, one could witness three services (10:00 a.m.; 12:00 p.m.; and 6:00 p.m.) with between to 1,900 to 2,100 people in attendance every weekend. By definition, Hillsong San Francisco was a megachurch.[1] Then the pandemic hit and Hillsong San Francisco found itself languishing in the wind of anonymity due to its inability to execute what it does best: Sunday services. The church drifted into a liminal space of uncertainty and abstraction unable to maintain its presence of relevance, unable to embody its belief of perpetual and ongoing triumphalism, and incapable of speaking to the pain and suffering many were experiencing—on a multitude of levels due to social and physical distancing or the death of loved ones—due to the church's inability to lament.

Frank Newport, in a news article for Gallup in April 2020, wrote, "The central organizational pattern of most modern religions in the U.S. is group

1. Allen Kim, "What is a Megachurch?"

worship, which has temporarily for the most part been mandated out of existence. The most dramatic result has been the exceedingly quick shift of religious services from in-person to virtual, online worship."[2] Many churches were uncertain in how to respond effectively as no one could be certain how long these measures would last. The creative practice of what one knew to be the church gathered, was assigned to a practice that was foreign, isolated, and disembodied. Local churches, faith leaders, and their communities were hoping for a swift turnaround and a return to normalcy. Little did people know that the COVID-19 pandemic would last more than eighteen months, and that many churches would, at worst, close or to varying degrees return with a community a fraction of its pre-pandemic population.[3]

Almost overnight, the church had shifted away from a public gathering of believers with a universal open door—Hillsong California and its three campuses were not immune to this reality. The COVID-19 pandemic shifted the locus and focus of the church and challenged its overarching theology and witness. The pandemic changed people's practical engagement with the local church. "In July 2020, roughly four months after COVID-19 upended life in America, 13% of U.S. adults reported having attended religious services in person during the previous month. That figure rose to 17% in March 2021 and then to 26% in September 2021, and as of March 2022 that now stands at 27%."[4] These oscillating, yet seismic, shifts in the body of the church impacted to varying degrees people's relationship with God, their family, and their faith community. As the mandates specific to social distancing and in-person church attendance assuaged, followers of Jesus in North America lamented, grieved, and mourned the deadly impact of COVID-19[5] and the loss associated with this deadly pandemic.

Similarly, faith leaders, pastors, and other Christians of influence seem to be wishing for a return to normal—a return to pre-pandemic practices—without seemingly seeking to implement any new, reimagined, theological, or social frame learned from almost two years in isolation. It seemed, especially for Hillsong California, that the leadership had quickly forgotten any creative, theological lessons from the coronavirus pandemic.

2. Newport, "Religion and the COVID-19 Virus," para. 1.

3. Kinnaman, "Year Out."

4. Nortey, "More Houses of Worship," para. 5.

5. During the final draft of this paper, the United States had experienced more than 1,003,570 deaths due to COVID-19. No doubt this number will continue to grow by the time this paper is graded. For the latest statistics regarding cases, positivity rates, hospitalizations, patients in ICU, and deaths, see "Track Covid-19 in the U.S."

The pandemic, albeit catastrophic for many people throughout San Francisco, was a creative theological opportunity for the church. Yet, many have since returned to a praxis, witness, and ecclesiology enamored with triumphalism, without necessarily learning from the liminality of the pandemic and the theological reflection that comes with lament and uncertainty.

Attending to Wounds

A symptom of triumphalism, combined with hyper-individualism, within North American evangelical churches, fails to attend to the wounds and grief of one's neighbor and their community. The narratives of lament and perpetual triumphalism are incompatible and irreconcilable as they fail to speak to the need, focus, and locus that is synonymous to each storyline and theology. A narrative of lament bears witness to one's neighbor, holistically embracing their moments of pain and sorrow, attending to the heart of their discomfort with empathy and compassion. Conversely, a narrative of triumphalism suppresses pain, isolates, and reduces one's interpretation of peace and flourishing as individual and financial, and fails to engage with the social issues of one's locality as an integral practice of peacemaking as the mission of God.

Weems writes, "The lament-complaint, perhaps Israel's most characteristic and vigorous mode of faith, introduces us to a 'spirituality of protest.' That is, Israel boldly recognizes that all is not right in the world. This is against our easy gentile way of denial, pretending in each other's presence and in the presence of God that 'all is well,' when it is not."[6] Lament is able to hold in tension the fallibility of this world, one's imperative to engage with it directly, and continually petition God to show up and intervene. At the same time, God is seeking those on mission with God to engage directly and consistently be God's hands and feet in local spaces and places—not just in church on a Sunday morning.

Lament is simply not taken seriously as fundamental practice of formation in the church. This is due, in part, to a thin, reduced, and hyper-ecstatic theology that asserts it is best to be blessed. "When lament is taken seriously . . . the practice issues in a crisis in God's sovereignty. . . . The lament over Israel's exile is a lament about YHWH's action as well as about the action

6. Weems, *Psalms of Lament*, vix

of my enemies (Lamentations 3:52). Indeed, it is the lament of Israel that evokes an admission from YHWH about abandonment (Isaiah 54:7–8)."[7]

It seems that a dramatic shift is required for lament to be seen, recognized, and embedded as a common theological practice in evangelical spaces. Theological interpretation and its associated practice is often framed by those in power. This forms a specific and unique culture in which the Bible is taught, and people are formed. Soong-Chan Rah, in *Many Colors: Cultural Intelligence for a Changing Church*, defines culture as "shared (collective within society), socially learned knowledge, and patterns of behavior."[8] He continues to outline culture as "acquired knowledge, lived experience, that helps you navigate the society you live in and provides guidelines for your interactions with others."[9] The culture of evangelicalism, which Hillsong San Francisco preserves, fails to see the impact that a lament-less culture has on its community. Post-pandemic, the church is less than 10 percent of its pre-pandemic population. For a multitude of reasons, people left the city, moved churches, or became part of a growing community in the Bay Area known as the dechurched. To be culturally intelligent, in a context like San Francisco and the Bay Area, is to adopt a learning posture to its history, become sensitive to the city's dynamic expression, seek to speak the local language (this may mean having a Spanish or Mandarin language service if necessary), and ensuring a multiracial, non-masculine expression of Christianity that includes intentionally the lost language of lament. Evangelical culture has failed to attend to the wounds of its people due mostly to its lament-less theological frame.

Miroslav Volf asserts, "We miss the mark if we believe that Christ's suffering somehow encourages the abused passively to accept their abuse."[10] Lament shifts the power from the center of the cultural community where white, male narratives dominate, to the margins, requiring many to shift their aligned understanding, praxis, and interpretation of the gospel from this dominant metanarrative to one that originates from below. This repositioning is what it means to be attentive to another's wounds. "In the context of standing with and lamenting on behalf of a suffering community, the understanding of the cross must start from below.[11] Those in evangelical

---

7. Lee and Mandolfo, *Lamentations in Contemporary Cultural Contexts*, 227.

8. Rah, *Many Colors*, 23.

9. Rah, *Many Colors*, 23.

10. Volf, *End of Memory*, 117.

11. Tesfai, *Scandal of a Crucified World*, 5.

circles must begin learning from and continuing learning with those on the margins of our local community. In the context of San Francisco, this includes our Asian American Pacific Islander (AAPI) sisters and brothers; LGBTQIA+ family; the city's homeless and underemployed community; and the local Ohlone indigenous community that includes the Chochenyo, Karkin, Ramaytush, Yokuts, and Muwekma people that populated the Bay Area well before colonizers occupied their land.

This learning and knowledge is imperative to the salvation of God's people in the city and the presence of a culture and theology of lament in the local church. Loida Martell-Otero, in *Latina Evangelicas: A Theology Survey from the Margins*, writes,

> Any soteriology that does not incorporate its radical call to serve those at the periphery is, in Dietrich Bonhoeffer's words, "cheap grace." It is disincarnate Christianity that allows its adherents to exploit the poor, ignore the suffering, and smugly await a heavenly reward at no cost to them. Only a soteriology of the privileged can ignore God's call to go "outside the gate." This is why the locus of salvation is never at the centers of power, which are blind to the inherent sin of injustice. To truly experience God's salvation, one must begin at the periphery, where *Jesús sato* beckons us to follow.[12]

Learning to attend to the city's wounds involves the posture and practice of lament. If it remains marginal to its practice, the church may recognize itself become more marginal to the city.

Unlearning Speed

Speed kills. Moving too quickly and parsing over another's pain or grief fails to engage with the reality or sacrality of their experience. Katongole and Rice affirm,

> Lament views speed with pessimism. Lament slows reconciliation down because it sees the challenge of transformation not from the top but from the margins—indeed from the bottom. Lament teaches us to see the world from the standpoint of exile in Babylon, crucifixion outside of Jerusalem, mass graves in Kigali, abandoned people in the New Orleans Superdome after Hurricane Katrina— even from a small place as a long marriage falling apart while both

---

12. Martell-Otero et al., *Latina Evangélicas*, 49–50.

husband and while feel powerless to stop it. Transformation feels very different from the bottom."[13]

Lament requests that those who are experiencing and witnessing pain slow down and call attention to the calamity before them. It calls the people of God, on mission with God, to journey with greater degrees of attention—even to sit in silence—in the presence and company of a lamenting voice.

One cannot be in motion, take ground, or run ahead in the presence of lament. Lament seeks solidarity and reliability and attention as one cries out for God's presence, action, and power. But to do so effectively the church must slow down. It is possible to still journey and be a sojourner with another, without moving. Katongole and Rice write, "Lament calls us into a fundamental journey of transformation. If we are to follow the path this practice lays out for us, we have to unlearn three things: speed, distance, and innocence."[14]

The speed of the church can often leave people behind. At times this speed makes sense. God has given God's people an imperative to participate with Jesus has he builds his church (Matt 16:18) and to go make disciples of all nations (Matt 28:19–20). This expediency is a misunderstanding of the work of the people of God. The church is called to partner with God as God builds God's church. This means that God leads, builds, establishes, and consecrates. We, as God's people, merely follow at God's pace. Alan Kreider, in *The Patient Ferment of the Early Church: The Improbable Rise of Christianity in the Roman Empire*, highlights this nuance. He affirms,

> Christian leaders didn't think or write about how to systematize the spread of Christianity; they were not concerned to cover the world evenly with evangelistic efforts. Instead, Christians concentrated on developing practices that contributed to the habitus that characterized both Christians and Christian communities. They believed that when the habitus was healthy, the churches would grow. Their theology was unhurried—a theology of patience.[15]

Understood well, lament creates liminal, slow, uncertain, and patience-forming spaces. A community's theology not only becomes unhurried, they become non-anxious.

---

13. Katongole and Rice, *Reconciling All Thing*, 81.

14. Katongole and Rice, *Reconciling All Thing*, 79.

15. Kreider, *Patient Ferment*, 74.

Finding oneself in a liminal, slow, unhurried, and non-anxious space does not equate to the people of God remaining in uncertainty forever. "Human beings cannot exist in liminality for an indefinite period of time."[16] Lament gives people time to go beneath the surface with the other and so cultivate understanding and build deep relationships. "[Augustine] saw lament as dwelling on present sufferings and eschatological hope concurrently: 'lament for things of the present, sing of what is to come in the future. Pray about what already is, sing about what you hope for.'"[17] It also helps people see that God desires to hear their heart and suffers with them as much as God wants to celebrate with them. "At the most basic level is it a consolation to those who suffer to know that God suffers too and understands their situation from within."[18]

Lament slows a people down to the rhythm, flow, and patient move of God. It may be that the North American evangelical church has misunderstood speed as a fruit or designation of success. In actuality, one's slowness is more effective and more appropriate in representing the way of God. This could be why it was seen as dishonorable for people to run in first-century Palestine.

The Economics of Hope and Despair

Hope and despair in the Christian narrative must go hand-in-hand. They are not mutually exclusive. To hope in or for something does not occur at the expense of the reality of despair. The posture and practice of lament teaches the possibility and reality that hope and despair conjointly exist in the presence of the other. To lament is to hope. To lament is to trust. To lament is to recognize and speak to the despair that engulfs and consumes the common person. To hope and despair at the same time is part of what it means to be human. It is also a mark an individual's or community's maturity.

Examining this historically, one must look at the manner in which Martin Luther King Jr. held hope and despair hand-in-hand. During a speech to students at Stanford in 1967, King laments the existential reality of people of color, suffering in poverty, yet remaining in a country that offers immense opportunity. In the early lines of King's speech, he describes

16. Sang Hyun Lee. *From a Liminal Place*, 6.
17. Harper and Barker, *Finding Lost Words*, 10.
18. Fiddes, *Creative Suffering of God*, 31.

an existential binary woven within the fabric of America's cultural tapestry. King laments,

> But tragically and unfortunately, there is another America. This other America has a daily ugliness about it that constantly transforms the buoyancy of hope into the fatigue of despair. In this America, millions of work-starved men walk the streets daily in search for jobs that do not exist. In this America, millions of people find themselves living in rat-infested, vermin-filled slums. In this America, people are poor by the millions. And they find themselves perishing on a lonely island of poverty, in the midst of a vast ocean of material prosperity.[19]

There exists a zero-sum narrative in North American evangelicalism that seems to assert that hope cannot exist in the presence of despair. This binary functions in the mode of racism, misogyny, the prosperity doctrine, and the interpretation of generational sin. In evangelical circles, one could only be suffering, poor, or marginalized due to an oversimplification of the gospel framed within a binary of positivity or loss. They have placed their hope in the wrong thing(s). Those who do find wealth, prosperity, favor, and blessing do so because they did not doubt. They put their faith in God, served in church, remained faithful in their tithes and offerings, and reaped their full reward in kind. Neither of these zero-sum narratives are biblical nor do they create space for the liberating, dynamic reality of lament.

The economics of this narrative cannot be zero-sum. God is not a zero-sum God. God is our comforting witness when no one else knows about one's initial cancer diagnosis. God is helper when one has lost their job and cannot find new, meaningful employment that comes with a livable wage. God is attentive to our cries when we have nowhere else to turn. God helps in our deepest moments of sadness when we think we are at the end of ourselves. Kathleen O'Connor asserts, "Implied in Lamentations' dynamic of the comforting witness is a spirituality of attentiveness not merely to the beauty, possibility, and wonder of creation but to internal conditions and external realities that deny the world's beauty, dehumanize others, and diminish life on this earth."[20] God's tool of lament makes us brave when everything inside us tells us the opposite.

All in all, the narrative and ecclesiology of lament is antithetical to the presiding nature of North American evangelicalism. One can begin to see

---

19. King, "Other America," para. 3.

20. O'Connor, *Lamentations and the Tears*, 108.

how the posture, practice, and language of lament has become foreign to so many. Rah reflects on the practice of lament in evangelical circles. He writes,

> Even as evangelicals discover and recover these important biblical themes, many want to use these themes to grow their church or expand influence rather than participate in the enactment of God's justice. The term justice is too casually thrown about without the corresponding sacrifice. We want the popularity of being associated with justice activists, but we don't to lament alongside those who suffer. Instead of a justice that arises from the lament of the suffering, justice is misappropriated as a furtherance of the narrative of celebration. American Christin justice leaders are applauded for their self-sacrifice, which allows for a furtherance of Western exceptionalism and even exploitation of justice a career-building move. The uplifting of privileged individuals who use justice to expand their own influence serves a narrative of triumphalism rather than engaging the narrative of lament.[21]

This is why the reality of the cross does not always bring victory. Before resurrection Sunday, one must experience the depth of Good Friday and liminal, transformative emptiness of Easter Saturday. Elizabeth Conde-Frazier, in *Latina Evangélicas: A Theology Survey from the Margins*, writes, "The privilege of the cross is the privilege of loss: it is grief and tears because we do feel compassion, and from compassion flows Latinas' own praxis of obedience and love, of imagination and healing, so that the power of the resurrection is released. *Evanglicas* do not pray to be delivered form these pangs but rejoice because those who suffer with Christ are likewise glorified with him."[22] To lament is to be brave and courageous in the face of despair. It is God's way of asking us to bring everything to God, just as God has done it all for us.

God's Hiddenness

Lament is a dynamic expression of trust and hope, calling out from the depths of sorrow and despair. Lament declares that God can handle one's pain as one shouts, questions, demands, and pleads. Lament is a precursor to shalom, but only after one has experienced the liminal uncertainty of God's silence in the wake of humanity's pain. Katongole writes, "A closer

---

21. Rah, *Prophetic Lament*, 146–47.
22. Martell-Otero et al., *Latina Evangelicas*, 106.

look at Jeremiah's lament-saturated ministry reveals that his laments operate on at least four levels: (1) a social critique; (2) to mourn the covenant; (3) as a reflection of YHWH's tears; and (4) to announce the newness of restoration. These four provide an outline of the conditions or possibilities for peace (shalom) as Jeremiah understood it."[23] God often remains veiled during lament, but God's veiling should not be misunderstood for God's absence. For God is never absent. "During lament," Zuidgeest writes, "the experience of God's hiddenness is an integral part of Israel's faith, but in an acute crisis it is particularly painful."[24]

Lament taps into our social and prophetic imaginary in ways that no other practice or liturgy in Scripture can. Lament awakens us to the depth of God's love for us, while also exposing a secret that is not often expressed in church settings: all suffering is sacred. Lament also realigns and challenges our values. Values are important because they act as guardrails and guidelines in moment of discord and uncertainty. Susan David, in *Emotional Agility*, writes,

> Having a clear understanding of your values is critical to finding change and fulfilment. It's not just that values are nice things to have. Rather, research shows that values actually help us access greater levels of willpower and grit and safeguard us from negative social contagion. They also protect us from subconscious stereotypes and beliefs that limit us without our even know they're there—and yet can have a real, negative impact on our ability to faces challenges.[25]

When one wails, people in the presence of that individual cannot help but remain silent. Grief is the ultimate connector as well as advocate. "The church has also been called on to play an important role in the field of advocacy. What I mean is that the church must be courageous enough to stand alongside those who are weak and defend their cause."[26] It is what makes the people of God human. We all know what it means to suffer. It takes a brave, courageous individual to do so in the presence of others. It is that reality that one must recognize the imperative of the role of the church in moments of suffering.

---

23. Katongole, *Born from Lament*, 151.

24. Zuidgeest, *Absence of God*, 131.

25. David, *Emotional Agility*, 125.

26. Tesfai, *Scandal of a Crucified World*, 72.

Robinson concludes *Voices of Lament: Reflections on Brokenness and Hope in a World Longing for Justice* with the following benediction,

> God of weary years,
> God of silent tears,
> Thou who has brought us thus far on the way,
> Thou who has by Thy might
> Led us into the light
> Keep us forever in the path, we pray.
> Selah[27]

I hope that this book brings an awareness to the need and highlights the importance of grafting in the posture, practice, and lost language of lament into evangelical spaces and places. Such awareness would not only challenge the status quo but also the toxic narrative that affirms a hyper-triumphalism that is not aligned with the gospel of Jesus.

---

27. Robinson, *Voices of Lament*, 249.

13

San Francisco and Lament

Teaching and learning are essential to civic well-being

—Rabbi Naham Ward-Lev

The ministry challenges of San Francisco and the Bay Area are confronting in themselves. San Francisco is not the most conducive environment for church planting, church renewal, or even church flourishing. As
noted, San Francisco has the smallest churchgoing population in the United
States. Sixty-one percent of the population of San Francisco in 2017 did not
attend church and one-third of all residents claim no religious affiliation.[1]
This is not only true for the city but is consistent throughout the Bay Area.
The Bay Area in 2017 was described as the most dechurched region in the
United States.

In an ecosystem where Christian practice and affiliation finds its back
up against the wall, it may seem counterintuitive to implement a practice
of formation that seeks to understand, explore, and embed lament into
its daily theology and practice. On the other hand, this theo-practical approach, framed around the theology, teaching, and theopraxis of lament in
the lives of faith leaders who call San Francisco home seeks to slowly and
intentionally equip the people of God, on mission with God, with a practice
that cultivates courage, hope, trust, and proximity.

1. "Church Attendance Trends."

Lament is a tool of hope for the flourishing and formation of the people of God in a city that has growing and ongoing demands, stresses, and anxieties. Many evangelical communities in San Francisco hope to provide speech and language to one's experience in courageously confronting God with the pain, sorrow, and grief in their lives. Singing, praise, and thanks are tools of worship and speech the church uses to express joy and wonder to God. Lament is also a tool of worship; when used correctly, it assists the lamenter with specifically targeted speech aligned to their suffering. This speech, when understood well, helps people imagine an alternative future[2] in the presence of God. When one comes against moments of hardship, sorrow, grief, and pain one does not need to be paralyzed by one's emotional response. Instead, lament helps one move towards God and seek God's involvement, healing, and presence where God often seems to be absent and silent.

Dan Allender affirms correctly that the church has "misunderstood the great value of public and private lament."[3] Allender continues, "Sanctification is a lifetime process of surrendering as more and more intense conflicts with God and others expose and dissolve our urgent preoccupation with the self. A lament is the battle cry against God that paradoxically voices a heart of desire and ironic faith in his goodness."[4] The ultimate purpose of this exploration is for the people of God, in San Francisco, to learn to lament in prayer and worship, publicly and privately, if our narrative of and engagement with God is to change. The North American evangelical church needs and requires this the transformation if it is going to remain faithful to its calling. Allender asserts,

> If we wish to invite a dying culture, one that flirts with knowing life is neither easy nor good, to consider the gospel, then we must learn to sing songs that face life with both honesty and hope. We need to learn to lament. We will consider the language of lament and the place for lament: the community of God.[5]

Living a life centered in Christ in San Francisco requires a renewed social imaginary. It asks the people of God to consider how life functions in the midst of suffering, pain, struggle, and loss . . . and then how we respond to it. This ministry project is not only an awareness raising activity, but also (as a secondary goal) a character forming one.

2. Brueggemann, *Prophetic Imagination*, 64.

3. Allender, "Hidden Hope in Lament," para. 7.

4. Allender, "Hidden Hope in Lament," para. 9.

5. Allender, "Hidden Hope in Lament," para. 10.

What lament has taught us is that life is not always about the context in which we find ourselves—the money we earn, the bodies we have, the places we live, or even the food we eat. All of this is important, but it is also peripheral. Lament has taught us that it is about our response to that context that is most important. How one responds in moments of joy, grief, wonder, victory, or sadness is imperative to one's walk with Christ. One's response, then, becomes the fulcrum that helps change a narrative and form a character that is aligned the way God has called God's people to live in the world—being shalom-makers in all areas of life.

Applying Lament as a Practice of Formation

The North American evangelical church needs and requires this transformation if it is going to seek to remain faithful to its calling. It asks the people of God to consider how life functions in the midst of suffering, pain, struggle, and loss . . . and how we respond. This ministry project is primarily an awareness raising activity, but also a character and community forming pursuit.

I am a life-long educator by trade and have been in church ministry and the education industry, teaching adolescents and adults for over twenty years. This exploration does have an intentional leaning towards and emphasis on pedagogical design, deep reflection, bridge-building and assimilation, and practical application.

This project began with a set of orientation questions for those who volunteered to participate. The design is in the shape of a pilot program, seeking ongoing and repeated feedback as a means of improving its impact and deep learning as volunteers participate in the learning journey.

This ten-month journey began with a set of orientation questions looking to establish a platform of prior knowledge and framed language around the subject of lament that seemed suitable to the context of San Francisco. The complete outline of orientation questions can be found in the appendix.

This small group of volunteers who came together all needed to satisfy a small number of requirements: (i) call San Francisco home; (ii) be leading a small group/connect group/Bible study for at least twelve months; (iii) live within a twenty mile drive of their current church location; (iv) be willing to commit to a twelve month pilot program; (v) be willing to commit to two meetings/month—once in person over dinner and once virtually over Zoom.

Guidelines and Boundaries

The group that finally assembled agreed that some of the content and topics shared would need to remain confidential. All names were redacted, and all participants agreed not to share any details of the content or stories people shared. As we began this journey together, we agreed that we would pray with and for one another. As a practical step towards this, participants were paired-off in groups of three to form prayer triplets. These prayer triplets would meet together at the beginning of each gathering to pray for one another. This was a fifteen to twenty minute practice.

Secondly, the group acknowledged and agreed that we would all seek to come into the pilot group with a posture of humility, recognizing our own brokenness and need for God. We agreed on four truths, which have been adapted in Dan Allender's book, *Leading with a Limp*: (1) we are never sufficiently good, wise, or gifted to make things work on our own; (2) my own failures may cause harm to others, the process, and myself, no matter how hard I to avoid failure; (3) the greatest I can do to myself or to others is try to limit the damage I caused by not participating, by quitting, by ignoring, or by pushing for complete control; and (4) calling out for help from God and others is the confession of humility and best recognition I know to show that I am still here.[6]

Lastly, as mentioned before, whenever we met in person, we met over food. We recognized and agreed that food helped our relationships become deeper, conversations richer, hangriness subside, and provided a willingness to continue in this journey of knowledge, formation, and practice grow.

Participants

The pilot group who came together to explore the theology, posture, and practice of lament and hope to raise awareness of and reflect on its need in our community consisted of nine participants who met the preset requirements The participants came from the following contexts and backgrounds. There are five female and four male participants. Four of the nine participants identify as collectively white (I used this term because I recognized that the term white failed to differentiate people's background, heritage, and cultural frame). Interestingly, none of the participants identified as being born and raised in San Francisco or the Bay Area. All had migrated to the

6. Dan Allender, *Leading with a Limp*. (New York, NY: WaterBrook, 2008), 71–72.

city within the previous seven years. Two participants identified themselves as AAPI, one Latinx, and two as Black/African American. All of the participants identified as heteronormative and either male or female—no participants self-identified as LGBTQIA+. Three of the nine participants did not grow up in Christian households, while three participants had spent the majority of their formative years outside the United States: Australia, Singapore, and El Salvador.

Only one member of the group had ever been to seminary or Bible college. All members of the group were full-time professionals. Seven out of nine had graduate degrees, and 66 percent of participants worked in the tech industry. Five of the participants are married (two to each other—meaning one couple) and all married participants have children under the age of three. The average age of male participants is 38, while the median is 36. The average age of female participants is 35.4 years, while the median age is 33.

The hope, despite this being a small pilot group, was to create a cross-section of participants that represented the city of San Francisco as appropriately as possible. While Hillsong San Francisco does have a majority population who identify as white, there is agreement that the racial make-up of the church does not replicate the racial make-up of the city.

Readings

The design of this group was to read one book a month specific to and around the theme of lament, grief, or sorrow, and then explore, reflect, create, and apply these learnings in one another's lives. As this project is designed to run for ten months, ten books were chosen help introduce and build an understanding of this topic. These resources are:

1. Emmanuel Katongole and Chris Rice. *Reconciling All Things: A Christian Vision for Justice, Peace, and Healing.* Downers Grove, IL: InterVarsity Press, 2008.

2. Sang Hyun Lee. *From a Liminal Place: An Asian American Theology.* Minneapolis, MN: Fortress Press, 2010.

3. Kathleen M. O'Connor., *Lamentations and the Tears of the World.* Maryknoll, NY: Orbis Books, 2002.

4. Soong-Chan Rah. *Prophectic Lament: A Call for Justice in Troubled Times.* Downers Grove, IL: InterVarsity Press, 2015.

5. Shelby Forsythia. *Permission to Grieve: Creating Grace, Space, and Room to Breathe in the Aftermath of Loss.* Chicago, IL Shelby Forsythia, 2019.

6. Grace Ji-Sun Kim and Graham Hill. *Healing our Broken Humanity: Practices for Revitalizing the Church and Renewing the World.* Downers Grove, IL: InterVarsity Press, 2018.

7. Emmanuel Katangole. *Born from Lament: The Theology and Politics of Hope in Africa.* Grand Rapids, MI: Eerdmans 2017.

8. Chanequa Walker-Barnes. *I Bring the Voices of my People: A Womanist Vision for Racial Reconciliation.* Grand Rapids, MI: Eerdmans, 2019.

9. Mark Charles and Soong-Chan Rah. *Unsettling Truths: The Ongoing, Dehumanizing Legacy of the Doctrine of Discovery.* Downers Grove, IL: InterVarsity Press, 2019.

10. David P. Gushee and Reggie L. Williams *Justice and the Way of Jesus: Christian Ethics and the Incarnational Discipleship of Glen Stassen.* New York, NY: Orbis Books, 2020.

The purpose of this monthly reading list is to provide a diverse range of voices, perspectives, and insights that do not merely come from a white, male, euro-centric perspective. This design is purposeful as many evangelical leaders in North America rely on or source predominately white, male voices.[7] The book choices raise awareness of the narrative and emphasis of peripheral voices that have often been muted or marginalized, bringing them to the table, so their insights and wisdom can more appropriately form the people of God.

As a concrete practice of breaking white cultural captivity of the North American evangelical church, of the twelve collective authors in the list above, seven are people of color, six are women, six are men; and five self-identify as white. While more books and many voices could have been added to this list, the goal of the pilot program ministry project was merely awareness raising.

The overarching narrative of the white cultural captivity of the church is too big, runs too deep, and has a long history that is far too wide to tackle, challenge or subvert in one pilot project. This is more of a survey of lament and its possible public ethic and application in the city of San Francisco and the theological DNA of the City.

7. Wallace, "White American Christianity."

Timeline

As stated earlier, at the writing of this book we are five months into a ten-month initiative. Due to people's commitments, this project began in January 2023 and will run for six consecutive months until the end of June 2023. Participants will then take one month off and read two books over the summer, returning in August 2023. This group aims to finish in October 2023, just prior to Thanksgiving—the entry point into the busiest time of the church calendar year.

At the end of the pilot project, participants will engage with an exit survey that seeks to focus and frame their learning, growth, and understanding as a counterpoint to their understanding at the beginning of this program. All participants agreed to purchase their own version of the readings and, when we meet in person, we agreed that one of us would host the in person meeting. This meant that each participant agreed to host once. We engaged in a potluck style meal with the explicit detail of bringing a dish that showed a deep significance to our personal history and tradition or a story that was linked to the dish that we would share as we ate together.

Goals for a Theopraxis of Witness

Kathleen O'Connor writes, "To gain a voice means to come into the truth of one's history corporately and individually, to recover one's life, to acquire moral agency by naming one's world."[8] To cultivate a theopraxis of witness, one must believe and be courageous in voicing their pain. This cannot always, and at times may not be wise to, be expressed in corporate settings. But it is imperative that one can do so in private settings. The first goal of a theopraxis of witness is that one needs to be brave enough to speak to God personally about their pain, bringing their grief and sorrow to God's attention.

O'Connor continues, "Just as denial in the garden pollutes relationships with self, others, the earth, and God [as a representation of the distortion of shalom], so denial in personal life directly affects social and political life. Despite the sharp dualism that separates personal and social life in Western cultures, boundaries between the two realms are porous."[9] The second goal of this project is that participants would no longer perceive life in a dualist way, framed by the beliefs of Western society. To be non-dualistic

---

8. O'Connor, *Lamentations and the Tears*, 83.

9. O'Connor, *Lamentations and the Tears*, 87–88.

recognizes that one cannot compartmentalize their life but must witness to the reality that everything in life, their wins and losses, ups and downs, income and expenditures influences everything else. If one is unable to speak to God personally about their pain and so bring their grief and sorrow to God's attention, they will be unable to move from a dualist orientation and relationship with the world, and towards a holistic orientation and interaction with God and God's creation.

Thirdly, O'Connor affirms a nuance that is imperative to all aspects of one's life, their relationships, their possible ministry, and their engagement with themselves. She writes,

> Without the knowledge of our own pain, and no matter our good intentions, we make objects of others. We treat them as we wish to be treated, not as they need and desire to be treated. We determine what is good for them, not they. . . . We callously disregard their suffering because it frightens us too much or because we do not perceive our connections to them. These dynamics appear in family life, friendships, and discipleship of mission and ministry. Lamentations beckons us to confront our own despair for our own sake and for the sake of the world.[10]

While I recognize this project is not and should not function as counseling group, participants have and will continue to engage directly with their own history of pain and suffering, and will require greater support than what I, the pilot group, or a pastor can offer. When needed, participants will be encouraged to connect with a counselor should they see it as an appropriate next step. The third goal for this pilot project is, therefore, that participants learn to confront their own despair for their own sake and for the sake of the world they move in. This will help them build empathy, listen to the voices of the distressed, and recognize that all suffering is sacred.

Lastly, in Lamentations and the practice of lament, those afflicted require a comforting witness. This is often a liminal, awkward space where only the lamenter speaks. The witness sees the suffering for what it is, and they learn to not deny, twist, or spin it. No platitude is offered and no pursuit for a quick, happy ending is assured. O'Connor writes, "The witness has a profound and rare human capacity to give reverent attention to sufferers and reflect their own truth back to them . . . in the encounter with those who suffer, the witness undergoes conversion from numbed or removed observer

---

10. O'Connor, *Lamentations and the Tears*, 92.

to passionate advocate."[11] The final goal in cultivating a theopraxis of witness in this research project is as follows: participants learn to give reverent attention to sufferers and reflect their own truth back to them by sitting with the sufferer in their pain and learning to be a passionate advocate.

To witness another's pain and suffering is a discipline. It is a learned behavior. Rabbi Nahum Ward-Lev speaks of the way the people of God learned new habits and new practices in the Old Testament. The writer of Deuteronomy asserted that the posture of learning, their motivation, concentration, application, and cooperation with God was linked deeply to their desire to serve and honor God in their relationships. Ward-Lev writes, in *The Liberating Path of the Hebrew Prophets: Then and Now,*

> Deuteronomy and the Prophets teach that learning stands at the heart of Israel's relationship with God. Teaching and learning are essential to civic well-being. This is an extraordinary, creative reimagining of how a community can flourish. Instead of attributing the inequities of the society to the sinful nature of the people, these texts perceive injustice and idolatry of Israelite society as a sign of a failure to learn, an indication of a need for more teaching. Sinful behavior is not innate to people's nature, but rather a product of bad learning.[12]

The theology, posture, and practice of lament along with Lamentations teaches us that who we are and how we engage with another's pain in the world does not have to remain that way. This is why, for all these goals in this research project, learning to give reverent attention to and so become passionate advocates of those experiencing all forms of pain and grief is a liberating exercise and experience for all involved. It brings people closer together. In this built proximity we learn to carry one another's pain and find ourselves in one another's story.

These four goals help focus and frame the posture, practice, and learning of lament these foreign evangelical spaces and places. To summarize, the four goals that hope to evident in the lives of all participants at the end of this research project are as follows:

1. Participants are brave enough to speak to God personally about their pain and bring their grief and sorrow to God's attention.

---

11. O'Connor, *Lamentations and the Tears*, 100.

12. Ward-Lev, *Liberating Paths*, 25.

2. Participants would no longer perceive life in a dualist way, framed by the beliefs of Western society.

3. Participants learn to confront their own despair for their own sake and for the sake of the world they move in.

4. Participants learn to give reverent attention to sufferers and reflect their own truth back to them by sitting with the sufferer in their pain and learning to be a passionate advocate.

14

Lament, Formation, and Community

A Formation Model

> When denial becomes a hardened way of life,
> it inhibits human flourishing...
>
> —Dr. Kathleen O'Connor

THROUGH THIS WORK I planned and framed that the group of participants meet together twice per month, once in person, once virtual. As a tool for helping busy people learn, I created and synthesized a learning model that helps bring learners on a predictable journey of formation, while also differentiating for each participant's needs as they grow, learn, apply, and reflect on the posture, practice, and theology of lament.

I seek through this learning model to help the participant bring any form of prior learning to the table. It is designed to be reflection rich, for it is in the moments of reflection that one grows, adapts, applies, and discusses one's experiences (see figure 2). As lament is not only a theology and posture, and most importantly a practice, the synthesis of this framework to a learning model of and for personal and communal formation is fundamental to the experience of these participants. This framework has been and continues to be used each time the group meets.

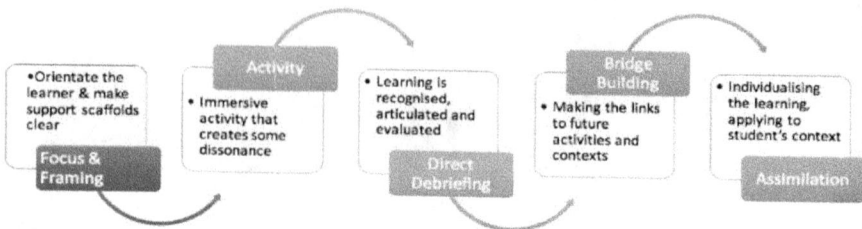

•Orientate the learner & make support scaffolds clear	Activity • Immersive activity that creates some dissonance	• Learning is recognised, articulated and evaluated	Bridge Building • Making the links to future activities and contexts	• Individualising the learning, applying to student's context
Focus & Framing		Direct Debriefing		Assimilation

Figure 2: A Formation Model

(Adapted from Schenck and Cruickshank, 'Evolving Kolb: Experiential Education in the Age of Neuroscience,' *Journal of Experiential Education* 2015, Vol. 38(1) 73–95.)

Figure 2 outlines the general flow of learning. When participants come together the agreed expectation has been that they have all read and completed, ideally, the whole book. One individual is tasked with providing an outline of the book and three key ideas that jumped out at them as they completed their reading. This is the focus and framing aspect of the above model.

The activity is the ongoing discussion and any practical steps that may be found in each book. For example, in *Permission to Grieve: Creating Grace, Space, and Room to Breathe in the Aftermath of Loss* by Shelby Forsythia there are numerous pause buttons and reflection questions throughout. Some include: "What if grief is a part of your life path, and not an obstacle to overcome?; What would happen if you embraced your grief emotions . . . instead of abandoning them?; How can you experience, recognize, and allow your feelings through permission granting?; What feeling can you give yourself permission to feel right now?"[1]

During the direct debriefing stage, participants are asked what they have learned by ways of articulating, recognizing, and evaluating. It is here that all participants are given the freedom and space to speak, listen, and hear one another. The gap between each meeting is intentionally designed as a break for reflection and adaption in one's life. It is here one may share their learnings with family and/or friends, may ask for prayer in their prayer triplet, or may personally practice lament.

1. Forsythia, *Permission to Grieve*, 93.

Returning to the group context, from the beginning of the second meeting, all participants were asked the same bridge building question: "How did you see your thinking, seeing, or doing change in light of lament over these past few weeks?" Here participants speak to and reflect on their formation. They are encouraged to journal or take video blogs throughout the week so they can share them with the group each time we meet in person.

Lastly, participants are given an active learning challenge designed as a way of going out into the world and experimenting with the learning. This is the final piece of the formation model: assimilation. This is where they individualize the learning and apply it to their context. Participants are asked to practice lament and journal their experiences. In doing so, assimilation becomes a character forming and habit inducing practice, not merely a principle. Below is the same model just reimagined as a spiral of learning, not just a flow of formation (figure 3).

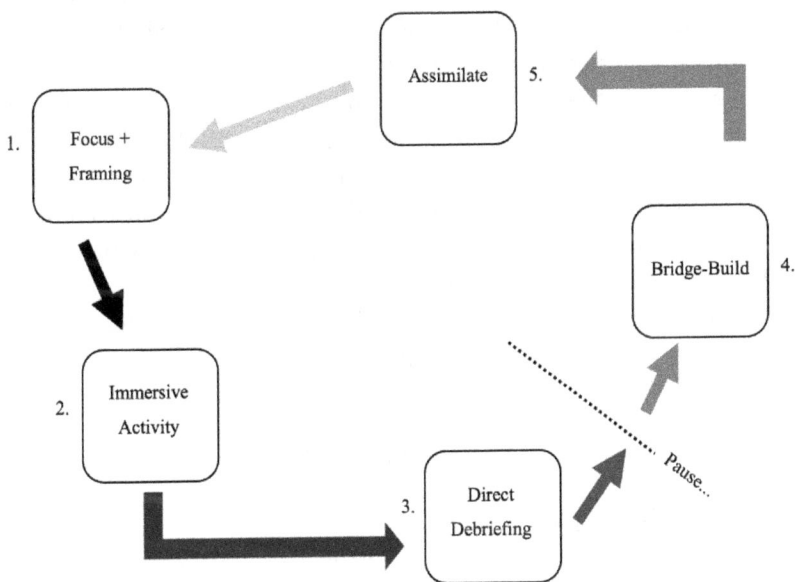

Figure 3: A Formation Model

(Adapted from Schenck and Cruickshank, 'Evolving Kolb: Experiential Education in the Age of Neuroscience,' *Journal of Experiential Education* 2015, Vol. 38(1) 73–95.)

This model is designed to be adaptable and contextual to the needs of participants and the perceived need of the city. It provides space for the Spirit to move in all God's fullness, while cultivating community and proximity within an intentionally scaffolded, yet unforced, gracious way.

In this chapter I evaluate and assess the relative impact of this research project at the half-way point of its implementation. Such evaluation and assessment focuses and frames the relative entry points of the participants and attempts to provide a narrative around this project's formative influence, shaping and understanding of lament in personal and public spaces and places. I also discuss my hope for the future as my project enters its final phase and culmination.

As seen in the appendix, all participants engaged with an orienting, introductory survey. This was primarily designed and aligned to the Likert scale where a score of one represented strongly disagree to the statement and a score of five represented strongly agree to the statement. Participants were given the opportunity to contribute their original definition of lament as well as their perception of three key attributes that make a just, impactful, and Christlike community effective in San Francisco. All responses remained anonymous with no identifying qualities attributed to any participant. Each participant in the survey signed a letter of consent that allowed for the reporting of outcomes specifically and only this research project.

The results of this orienting, introductory survey is discussed below. In section one I frame questions around the theme: lament for the community. In section 2 I explore the theme: lament for the individual. In section 3 I survey the theme: lament as a praxis of justice.

Pilot Survey: Lament, Formation, and Community

In this section I explore three general questions on the Likert scale. The purpose of this section is to seek an orientation to the idea and concept of lament in general. Because the practice of lament can be quite jarring and personal, I did not want to begin with questions around lament as it may have caused too much dissonance for the participants.

One interesting data point from the initial survey was that sixteen people were initially interested in participating in the survey and research project. Despite initial support and words of affirmation, only nine people responded. Participation in the pilot project was conditional on completion of the introductory survey. Despite my curiosity as to why response rates not as encouraging as I had desired, I did not enquire as to why people did not engage in the initial process, despite their supportive and overwhelmingly generous affirmations and words of encouragement. To speculate, perhaps the subject matter was too confrontational. Perhaps, like many of us, people were simply too time-poor to engage fully in the project. Possibly there could have already been a high degree of dissonance when they read about the subject matter and did not want to go to a space or place intellectually, communally, or existentially and be vulnerable with their stories. Or, lastly, it could have been easier for some to believe that the best was yet to come instead of dealing directly with the thought of lament.

Orientation Lament Survey

Participants were initially asked, around the theme of lament for the community, three opening questions. The first question posed the statement "I believe my faith community has a sound understanding of the theology and practice of lament."

Table 1: Understanding of Lament

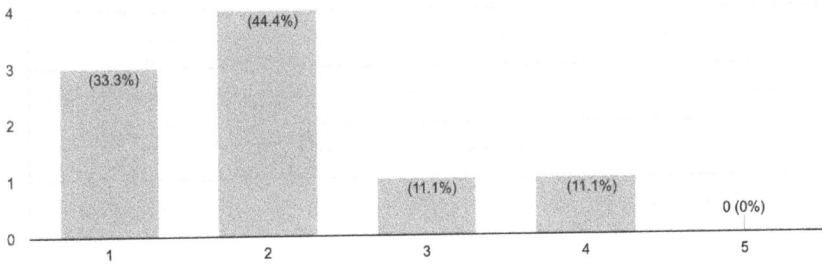

Participants were asked to assess the faith community's understanding and practice of lament. No participants strongly agreed that the church had a sound understanding of the theology and practice of lament. Responders either disagreed or strongly disagreed with the assertion around sound theology and practice of lament (77.8 percent). This is consistent with the themes presented by many theologians around the topic and theme of lament. The evangelical church of North America finds this to a difficult subject, practice, and theology to effectively engage.

The second question in posed the statement "I believe my faith community teaches lament well in corporate settings. Only 11.1 percent agreed with this statement, while the other responders either disagreed or strongly disagreed. From these responses, it truly does seem that lament is a lost language and foreign concept to many in the church. While this statistic does not represent the reality across all North American evangelical communities, it is symptomatic of the reality in San Francisco. The need for awareness raising around this theology, posture, and practice is imperative. If it is rarely taught in public, corporate settings, it becomes evident that it is not central to the cultural norms nor the expression of the community.

Table 2: Teaching Lament in Corporate Settings

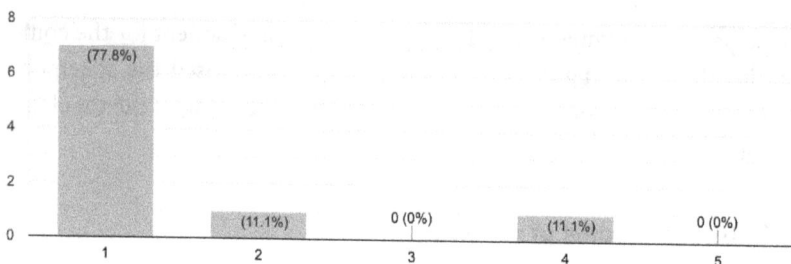

The third question in part explores the recognition and perceived importance of lament in the community's walk with Jesus. Essentially, it asks if lament plays a key role in one's daily walk with Christ. The responses were surprising. More than half of responders recognized the importance and need for lament in their life and walk with Christ. Yet, taken hand in hand with the cultural and theological context they were emanating from, they were not receiving it on a consistent enough basis to recognize its presence and teaching in their faith community (table 3).

Table 3: Daily Importance of Lament

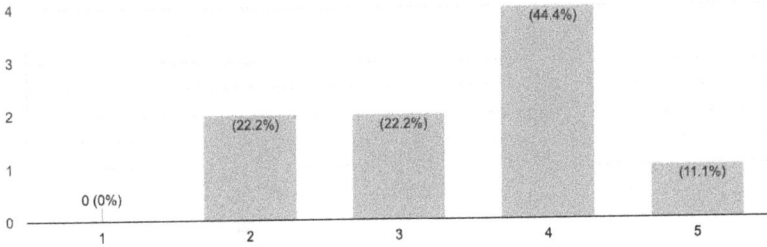

The next section moved from a communal understanding of lament to an individual perspective of lament. In this section, responders were asked four questions that explored their personal understanding of lament; their ability to define lament biblically; their perception if God can handle their grief or pain—if they were ever to lament to God; and, lastly, in moments of grief and despair, is it easier for them to believe the best is yet to come compared to engaging God in the practice of lament and articulating their feelings to God. Essentially, I wanted to see if there was a split between responders' intellectual understanding of and engagement with lament, compared to their willingness to practice it and place themselves in a context of vulnerability. The results were fascinating.

Initially, 55.6 percent of responders asserted they could define lament in a sound manner; 33.3 percent were not sure and chose to sit on the fence with the understanding. One responder asserted that they could not define it well (table 4).

Table 4: Ability to Define Lament

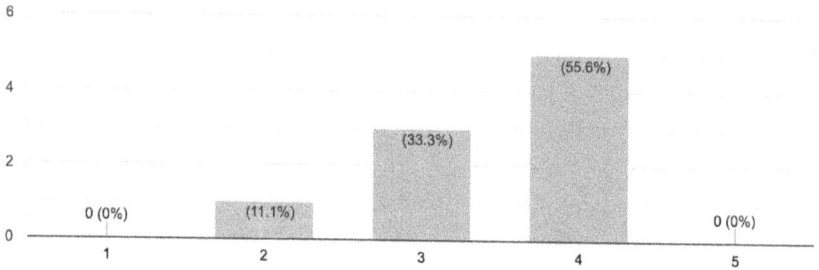

When it came defining lament, all responders were prompted to answer a number of the responses. One responder framed lament as "spiritual formation found on the journey of through grief and suffering." Another framed it as "to join God's grief and pain in the waywardness of creation and to join Christ's suffering and sorrowful time on earth. From these places, to be able to also sit in the pain and grief of other fellow beings and love them." I found the following response captivating and thoughtful:

> Lament is the process of accepting loss in one's life. I believe this is a practical way from an inward belief. What do I mean by that? Lament for me is a life decision to understand I don't have control of everything and that I will suffer pain and loss on Earth. As a believer of [sic] Jesus I know he has the victory as an outcome but during the process of life I am exposed to various issues that can cause pain in my life. All of us are not immune to suffering, but how we process it is different.

Lastly, another defined lament as "expressing your grief, anger, fear, and pain to God on experienced drama and events."

While many were not confident in their ability to define lament, most of the responders were able to name and define lament with relative degrees of success. I wonder what this could look like if lament was taught more consistently in our local faith community. I believe many more in the congregation and in the city of San Francisco would be equipped with a way of witnessing and expressing pain and suffering. I believe it would help build deeper relationships and help form greater degrees of proximity not only for Hillsong San Francisco, but for those who consider themselves locals but distal from the community. Lament would help contribute to the way people know and engage with church in a more formative, slow, and intentional manner.

When asked if people believed God could handle their grief and complaints, every responder agreed with a strongly agreed.

Table 5: Can God Handle Our Grief?

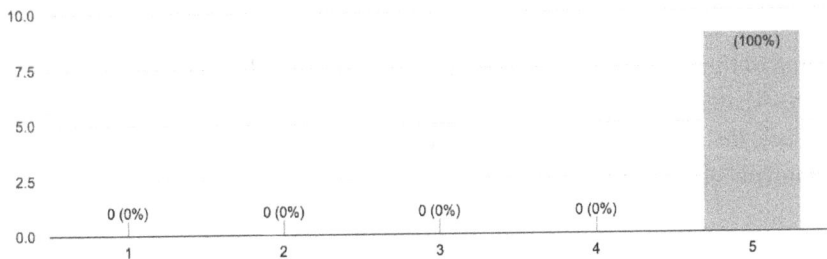

There was a clear disconnect between people's belief that God could handle their grief and pain, and their willingness to be vulnerable. Kathleen O'Connor speaks repeatedly about an ongoing denial in Western society. Such denial has led to increased use of medication as a response to anxiety which has, in turn, led to a growing dependency and addiction to prescription medication. O'Connor writes, "When denial becomes a hardened way of life, it inhibits human flourishing, cuts off the spirit at its roots, silences voices, and blocks passion for justice. Whether practiced in societies or individuals, denial constricts hope, depletes life, and aborts praise. Crushed spirits cannot worship unless that worship speaks from pain."[2] Her assertion seems to be accurate here.

When asked, "In moments of despair, loss, and/or grief, it is easier for me to believe 'the best is yet to come' than to lament and contend my feelings to God?" 66 percent of responders asserted disagreed. It was easier for them to lament to God than it was believe the best is yet to come. Still, 33 percent of responders were either not sure, or agreed. Each and every one of us are on a journey with Christ. To lament to God is to engage actively in a practice of trust and hope when everything surrounding us states otherwise. This set of responses make sense. It takes courage and bravery, nuanced with the type of pain someone is experiencing to lament to God.

The third and final section of this survey explored lament as praxis of justice. Five questions framed with the Likert scale sought initial thoughts

2. O'Connor, *Lamentations and the Tears*, 87.

and feelings. The first question asked responders to weave the theme of biblical justice within the practice of lament and assess its importance. As seen in table 6, 22.2 percent responses were unsure, 55.6 percent of those surveyed agreed, while there were two polemic responses amongst the group. There was not great consensus around this question. While 66 percent responded with either agree or strongly agree, such a smattering is emblematic of the church's position on matters of justice. To some, justice in public spaces and places is not imperative to the work Jesus. When it came to the reality of the COVID-19 pandemic and the presence of Black Lives Matter in the summer of 2020, churches that remained silent seemed to lack the theology and, possibly, willingness to lament clearly in these moments of communal uprising.

Table 6: Lament and Justice

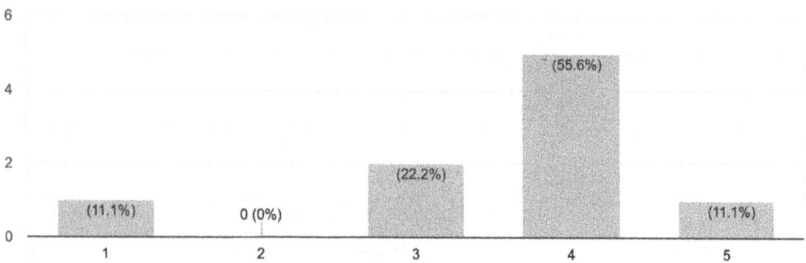

Lament, practiced authentically, is the appropriate right first step in any moment of public injustice. Be it around racialized violence, the death of family or friends due to the pandemic, or ongoing drug abuse on the streets of San Francisco, the people of God are called to first lament the grief of the city and demand God show up and act against the perpetrators of injustice.

Secondly, it was asked if the local church should focus on more things than just the spiritual health of the people. The question was purposefully left open-ended and open to interpretation. Eighty-eight percent of responded with either agree or strongly agree. People see that God asks us to do more; what that looks like and how it is practiced is the work of the people within the context of the city itself.

Table 7: More than Just the Spiritual Health of the People of the City

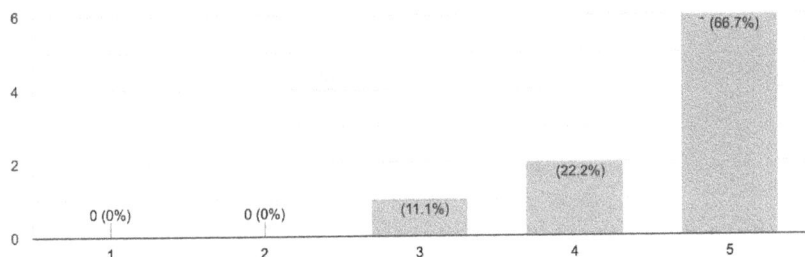

Thirdly, participants were asked in statement, "The weekly church service is the most important expression what it means to follow Jesus." North American evangelical communities in recent times have placed a strong emphasis on the production and focus of Sunday service. At times, one could argue, at the expense of any other aspect of the community. When people at Hillsong San Francisco are asked to serve, of the six main avenues of service—welcoming, guest relations, music team, sound and lighting, children's ministry, and operations—all six options to serve are service-centric. There are no creative serving options consistently available outside of a Sunday morning service. It seems that responders are aware of this reality but paralyzed to know how to change this narrative.

Lastly, in light of all these questions about lament, participants were asked to describe three elements that make a just, impactful, and Christlike community effective in San Francisco. Some responses were as accessible and direct as "Authentic Community, Shared Spiritual Disciplines, Intentional Rest, and Reflection"; another affirmed, "1. Intimacy with the Holy Spirit to discern the needs of San Francisco. 2. Commitment to living by the practices of Jesus (e.g., Rule of Life). 3. Holy fear of the Lord in obedience to fulfilling His purpose of creation." Again, another person affirmed, "I struggle to answer this question because 'effective' is predicated on the ultimate goal and how you measure success. There is a difference between what is effective for people like me vs. them. Additionally, after working with people in various states of addiction and/or mental health crisis, I question my notions of effective." This same responder later affirmed the elements,

133

"(1) Lacks selfish ambition, (2) Acknowledges experience/ community differences, (3) Exists in the spaces where people live."

These three responders gave disparate answers, yet all had one overlapping assertion. They all desired proximity in the form of community with God and within the people of the city. All responders desired a combination of embodied presence, community, or practices of hospitality. Anything that brings people together is at the heart of what these participants desired and who they seem to be hoping to become.

Focus and Framing

Within every session of the pilot group we engage with the framed readings and attempt to contextualize much of the discussion to specific issues, challenges, and opportunities within the city limits of San Francisco. We intentionally begin with our own immediate context, be it family, friends, one's marriage, someone's dating relationship, the demands of work, or other items that may be personal and pertinent to someone's need.

In alignment with the pilot project's model of formation, as participants move through each aspect of the model, they also engage specifically with the text and its ramifications to the practice of shalom. In essence, the practice of lament for many who participate in this research project has been the pursuit and cultivation of shalom in all areas of life: peace with God, peace with their neighbor, peace with their context or environment, and peace with themselves.

Each session explores five key questions as we move through the model of formation: (i) What have I learnt from this text that I was not aware of before I engaged with it? (ii) How can I apply this new learning to my daily walk with Jesus as I move about the city? (iii) Did I find it challenging when I first practiced this new understanding (if so, how)? (iv) Why do the people of San Francisco need what we are learning (and it what ways could we make it accessible to the city)? and (v) How can I remind myself to practice this new reality on a consistent basis?

The focus and framing of such questions help learners graft their prior knowledge to their new understanding and then contextualize it to their needs.

Key Practices

Cultivating practices are fundamental to the expression of following Jesus. For María Pilar Aquino, a Latinx Mexican American feminist theologian, the practice of hope "is not a far-off ideal or a palliative. It is a deep spiritual force—because it comes from the Spirit—that encourages the poor in their struggles. It is an objective reality, an anticipation of God's justice and love as experienced in the life, death, and resurrection of Jesus."[3]

The formation of a person or a people is found not merely in the change of heart, or in their behavior modification, but in a true, deep, formative, and Holy Spirit inspired transformation. It is a full renovation of mind, body, and spirit. It is an overflow that demonstrates the transformation of one's conviction in all areas of life and the pursuit of developing practices— similar to the development of liturgy—that helps people remember God in moments of despair.

The pursuit and theology of lament is not a principle in itself. It is a practice and way of being in the world. Lament in contexts and imperatives of public justice and communal hope demonstrate a people's spiritually mature response to sadness, violence, and grief. A church community's spiritual aliveness is found in its ability to bring these public injustices to God, a lament, in hope that God will show up and intervene and bring justice to an unjust world.

As such, this has resulted in a set of common, key practices that have been created out of and from this doctoral group. They became part of the group's liturgy, per se, and are fundamental to how we now meet and commune and pray.

We now begin by sharing a frustration, heartache, or pain that occurred between sessions. The group calls this our acknowledgement. We began to see, hear, and feel one another's burdens and heaviness from the week. We wanted to find a way to speak to our frustration without anyone unintentionally parsing over it with a platitude or word of assurance. We found this practice helped the group in a multitude of unexpected ways. Firstly, the person voicing their frustration was given permission and space to articulate what was on their heart in the fullest assurance that they could voice it all, without pushback; secondly, those hearing the acknowledgement learnt to sit in a liminal space. Sang Hyun Lee speaks of this effectively and many found his work to be highly impactful. For many, at first it

---

3. Aquino, *Our Cry for Life*, 73.

was difficult and frustrating. One person described as "having an itch that I wanted to scratch but knowing it would be better for me if I left it alone and experienced the fullness of its itchiness."

Next, we moved onto the book that we had read over the last month. When we came to our set of five questions as seen above, we redesigned the experience so one person walked through the five questions at once (in the first two in-person meetings, each person answered one question at a time which was slow and lethargic and did not allow people to develop their thoughts). I have appreciated the development of deeper thoughts and responses and have learned more from listening to these gatherings than I first anticipated.

Lastly, as we depart we ask ourselves the question, "What is God doing in San Francisco here and now?" It was an idea that originated from one of the participants as she wanted to see if any of the other participants would return the following month with a similar answer. She asked everyone to write it down before coming to the next gathering and use it as a way of seeing, hearing, and understanding the needs of the city and how God's Spirit is directing us.

Next Steps

In assessing the ongoing success of this project there is still much to do. I am excited that this group of people—who love Jesus, love the local church, and love the city of San Francisco—are creating new and dynamic practices themselves—practices that were not originally designed as part of the model of formation, central to cultivating a theology, posture, and practice of lament, or seen of as necessary to the cultivating of community and proximity to one another. From the initial survey results to the ongoing development of the group, God is slowly helping people challenge the presiding narrative of hyper-triumphalism that is endemic in the North American evangelical churches.

Participants are still keen to meet after the summer break and finish what they have started. The objectives of this research project have been achieved:

1. Participants were brave enough to speak to God personally about their pain and so bring their grief and sorrow to God's attention.

2. Participants would no longer perceive life in a dualist way, framed by the beliefs of Western society.

3. Participants learn to confront their own despair for their own sake and for the sake of the world they move in.

4. Participants learn to give reverent attention to sufferers and reflect their own truth back to them by sitting with the sufferer in their pain and learning to be a passionate advocate.

Ultimately, this pilot group raised the need for and awareness of the theology, posture, and practice of lament in the local church in San Francisco.

Summary and Conclusion

In moments of despair, we are reminded and
remember that God's love never fails

EMMANUEL KATONGOLE AND CHRIS Rice write, "To learn lament is to become people who stay near to the wounds of the world, singing over them and washing them, allowing the unsettling cry of pain to be heard."[1] Katongole and Rice, however, continue on and ask a provocative question: "Are we ready to become that vulnerable?"[2] It does seem that the elephant in the room and the silent theme in the background to this paper has been concerned with vulnerability. The church needs to be willing and able as the bride of Christ to become vulnerable in its interactions with others and coheirs with Christ.

The survey results and discussion demonstrated a desire and willingness to become vulnerable with one another. But this took time to grow and cultivate and establish as a norm. As one laments in this group, they open themselves up in vulnerable ways. There is the common allegory of windows and mirrors. Such a metaphor seems appropriate for the theology, posture, and practice of lament. The lamenter becomes a window and a mirror all at once. They are a window to their neighbor, the one sitting, seeing, hearing, and acknowledging their pain. They can see into their reality and understand their pain. As the lamenter voices their grief, I have come to learn that the ground they are standing on becomes sacred—like Moses when he was face-to-face with the burning bush. To lament to acknowledge

---

1. Katongole and Rice, *Reconciling All Things*, 94.
2. Katongole and Rice, *Reconciling All Things*, 94.

that suffering is sacred and requires a reply with silence as a form of love, reverence, and love.

The lamenter also becomes a mirror—for themselves and for the community they have witnessed to. Voicing their pain and injustice they bear witness to their own journey. A journey through pain and suffering, abuse and violence, racism and misogyny, cruelty and loss. To be a mirror of one's own lament is to see bravery in oneself, to place hope and trust in God when everything is ruined. To be a mirror of one's lament is to acknowledge that one matters—to God, to one's neighbor, and to oneself.

To be a mirror or a window in the moment of lament is the first, and often untold, step towards peacemaking and reconciliation. Chanequa Walker-Brown, in *I Bring the Voices of My People: A Womanist Vision for Racial Reconciliation*, writes,

> Any reconciliation that does not liberate and heal the oppressed from the consequences of oppression is not reconciliation at all. At best, its cheap grace [or cheap hope], an easy balm that offers forgiveness for the sin of White Supremacy without seeking to correct the harm it inflicted. At worst, it's an affirmation of White Supremacy in that it prioritizes the need for White people to feel better about their relationships with people of color over the needs of people of color to recover from the psychological and material impact of oppression.[3]

As the people of God on mission with God recognize their compliance in the ongoing breaking of relationships due to a lack of humility and courage to lament, and confess to God and one another, the church will continue to perpetuate the status quo, an easy balm that offers forgiveness for the sin without seeking to correct the harm it inflicted.

Implications for San Francisco, the Local Church, and the People of God

In one of the ongoing surveys, a respondent differentiated between three elements that make a good church and three elements that make a just and impactful church. They differentiated their response in this way,

> The three foundational elements of a Good church include, 1. Bible Centered Teaching: the ability to provide an understanding of and

---

3. Walker-Barnes, *I Bring the Voices*, 183–84.

encounter with the Christian faith through clear and accurate in-
terpretations of the Bible and how it can guide the church in our
daily lives; 2. Community Building: the ability to facilitate friend-
ship, mentorship, and social opportunity for its congregation. 3.
Community Serving: the ability to understand and contribute to
the local community with physical, financial, and timely resources.

As a counter point to the above, they premised their description of a just
and impactful church with the following caveat: "What makes a church just
and impactful is letting each and every action be guided by the needs of the
people, not personal ambition." Their explanation was as follows, "1. The
church needs to understand the community around them by listening to
their needs and hearing their cries, not simply telling them what they need;
2. The church needs people centered leadership that focuses on the church's
faithfulness to its community, not expecting the people to be faithful to the
church; and 3. A safe space for the hurting and broken."

What this person brings to the fore is a reimagination of the church
that asks its people to slow down so they can hear and see the cries of its
city and respond as the Spirit is prompting. It is the building of empathy.
Brené Brown describes empathy as "a strange and powerful thing. There is
no script. There is no right way or wrong way to do it. It's simply listening,
holding space, withholding judgement, emotionally connecting, and com-
municating that incredibly healing message of 'You're not alone.'"[4] Choos-
ing empathy is asking the church to slow down.

This is a scary thought for a movement of people who want their
churches to grow as fast as private organizations readying themselves for
the stock market and seeking profit margins similar to multinational cor-
porations. A slower church is a non-anxious community of people. It is a
people not in a hurry to grow, to move, or to act. The implications of and for
this is that the church adopts a listening and learning posture, where it lis-
tens attentively to when the word is read and preached, and they patiently
call to account how and when God is moving—then they move. "Their re-
flexes are non-violent [in thought, word, and deed] and when others treat
them violently, they never exact an eye for an eye but respond in silence and
patience, and even offer words of blessing."[5]

In San Francisco, many of the issues are overwhelming. No one can
contest the reality of the current poor, violent, drug-laden reality of the city.

4. Brown, *Daring Greatly*, 81.
5. Kreider, *Patient Ferment*, 19.

If one is trying to win the city for Christ, then the work is futile. There is no strategy in saying that a church will win the city for Christ. But there is in local faithfulness. Building relationships and hearing stories and learning the heartbeat of a city so that a people can learn about another group of people and effectively love them.

As this group continues towards the end of this calendar year, it has been suggested we begin to walk the city as one of our activities. By walking the city, we will begin to learn about its nuances, rhythms, and need.

A letter was sent to me late last week from the husband of one of the research project participants. He and his wife both attend the group and sent this feedback while at work.

> I have observed a change in the words my wife uses and need to commend you on this work. We are thankful for this opportunity and have benefitted from the insights of the book provided and stories shared. The teaching we have received has challenged our preconceived notions, broadened our perspective, convicted, and inspired us to be more like Jesus.
>
> For those who feel drawn to spend more time in the Bible, whether gleaning insight from the Bible makes you feel alive or you have questions about verses that seem to make no sense, this teaching will bring insight not previously considered.
>
> This group provided context, drew from historic and contemporary scholars and the original language. He welcomed discussion and questions regarding verses in the Bible that appear to clash with today's cultural norms. This group was able to draw our attention to Jesus' heart and intention of lament, to draw us closer together, to him, and to ourselves.

The power and practice of lament is truly beneficial and cathartic for all, those who lament and those who bear witness to the lamenter. To be truth-tellers in times of uncertainty is a blessing. Lament is a liminal enterprise with no known immediate closure. This is the beauty in trusting God. In moments of despair, we are reminded and remember that God's love never fails. It is this recalling and remembering that gives one the agency to create brave spaces of shared belonging, and so give themselves and others permission to grieve.

Appendix

Intro Survey

Permission to Grieve: Creating Space for Lament and Loss as a Theopraxis of and Witness

Introduction

THIS RESEARCH PROJECT INVITES followers of Jesus, living in San Francisco, to participate in an orientation survey as part of their initial participation in a twelve-month long pilot formation group exploring the theology, posture, and practice of lament in San Francisco.

The questions below vary in nature but have the common desire of gauging the theological status quo of the theology of lament and grieving taught, presented, practiced, and understood in Hillsong San Francisco. This introductory orientation survey will help inform our mutual understanding of lament, its current role in our lives, and its potential impact in the lives of those who call San Francisco home.

Many thanks, in advance, for your insights and contribution to this work.

Appendix

Part 1—Lament for the Community

A. I believe my faith community has a sound understanding of the theology and practice of lament.

1	2	3	4	5
Strong Disagree				Strongly Agree

B. I believe my faith community teach lament well in corporate settings.

1	2	3	4	5
Strong Disagree				Strongly Agree

C. I recognize that lament is an important part of my church's walk with Jesus.

1	2	3	4	5
Strong Disagree				Strongly Agree

Part 2—Lament for the Individual

A. I believe I can define and describe lament in a sound manner.

1	2	3	4	5
Strong Disagree				Strongly Agree

B. I would define lament as:

_____

_____

_____

_____

_____

C. I believe God can handle my grief and complaints:

1	2	3	4	5
Strong Disagree				Strongly Agree

D. In moments of despair, loss, and/or grief it is easier for me to believe, 'the best is yet to come' than to lament or contend my feelings to God.

1	2	3	4	5
Strong Disagree				Strongly Agree

Part 3—Lament as a Praxis of Justice

A. I understand lament to be an important aspect of biblical justice.

1	2	3	4	5
Strong Disagree				Strongly Agree

B. To have a more meaningful presence in the city of San Francisco, church communities need to contribute to the community in more ways than the spiritual health of the people.

1	2	3	4	5
Strong Disagree				Strongly Agree

C. The weekly church service is the most important expression of the community in what it means to follow Jesus.

1	2	3	4	5
Strong Disagree				Strongly Agree

D. The church is called it embody its calling by demonstrating the reign of God in all areas of city life.

1	2	3	4	5
Strong Disagree				Strongly Agree

E. Describe three elements that make a just, impactful, and Christlike community effective in San Francisco.

_____

_____

_____

_____

_____

_____

Bibliography

"About Hillsong." Hillsong Church, n.d. https://hillsong.com/about/.

"About Us." CCV, n.d. https://ccv.church/about.

"About Us."Lakewood Church, n.d. https://www.lakewoodchurch.com/about.

Allender, Dan. "The Hidden Hope in Lament." The Allender Center at the Seattle School, June 2, 2016. https://theallendercenter.org/2016/06/hidden-hope-lament/.

———. *Leading with a Limp*. New York, NY: WaterBrook, 2019.

Aquino, María Pilar. *Our Cry for Life: Feminist Theology from Latin America*. Maryknoll, NY: Orbis, 1993.

"Axiom." Merriam-Webster, n.d. https://www.merriam-webster.com/dictionary/axiom.

Baer, Drake. "Why Boundaries Are the Best Thing for Creativity." Fast Company, Mar. 3, 2014. https://www.fastcompany.com/3027070/why-boundaries-are-the-best-thing-for-your-creativity.

Billings, J. Todd. *Rejoicing in Lament: Wrestling with Incurable Cancer and Life in Christ*. Grand Rapids: Brazos, 2015.

Blaine-Wallace, William. *When Tears Sing: The Art of Lament in Christian Community*. Maryknoll, NY: Orbis, 2020.

Bonhoeffer, Dietrich. *The Cost of Discipleship*. New York: Touchstone, 1959.

———. *Ethics*. New York: Touchstone, 1995.

Bowles, Nellie. "How San Francisco Became a Failed City: And How it Could Recover." *The Atlantic*, June 8, 2022. https://www.theatlantic.com/ideas/archive/2022/06/how-san-francisco-became-failed-city/661199/.

Branson, Mark Lau, and Juan Martinez. *Churches, Cultures, and Leadership: A Practical Theology of Congregations and Ethnicities*. Downers Grove, IL: InterVarsity, 2011.

Brown, Brené. *Daring Greatly: How the Courage to be Vulnerable Transforms the Way We Live, Love, Parent, and Lead*. London: Penguin, 2012.

Brown, Robert McAfee. *Unexpected News: Reading the Bible with Third World Eyes*. Philadelphia: Westminster, 1984.

Brueggemann, Walter. *Peace*. Nashville: Chalice, 2001.

———. *The Prophetic Imagination*. 2nd ed. Minneapolis: Augsburg Fortress, 2001.

———. *Psalms of Lament*. Louisville: Westminster John Knox, 1995.

Bibliography

———. *Sabbath as Resistance: Saying No to the Culture of Now.* Louisville: Westminster John Knox, 2014.

Card, Michael. *A Sacred Sorrow: Reaching Out to God in the Lost Language of Lament.* Colorado Springs, CO: NavPress, 2005.

Carrington, Alexis, et al. "COVID-19 Pandemic Forces a Nationwide Reckoning for American Churches on How to Open Safely: Church Attendance Dropped During the Pandemic." ABC News, Feb. 26, 2022. https://abcnews.go.com/Health/covid-19-pandemic-forces-nationwide-reckoning-american-churches/story?id=82448256.

Castle, Toby. "Repentance, (Re)coniliation, and Restitution: The Posture and Practice of Peacemaking as the Mission of God." Paper, PR715 Preaching and Justice: Communication for Spiritual and Social Transformation, Fuller Theological Seminary, 2022.

Charles, Mark, and Soong-Chan Rah. *Unsettling Truths: The Ongoing, Dehumanizing Legacy of the Doctrine of Discovery.* Downers Grove, IL: InterVarsity, 2019.

Chatfield, Graeme R. *Finding Lost Words: The Church's Right to Lament.* Eugene, OR: Wipf & Stock, 2017.

Cho, Eugene. *Thou Shalt Not Be a Jerk: A Christian's Guide to Engaging Politics.* Colorado Springs, CO: David C. Cook, 2020.

"Church Attendance Trends around the Country." Barna, May 26, 2017. https://www.barna.com/research/church-attendance-trends-around-country/.

"City Care." Hillsong California, n.d. https://hillsong.com/usa/california/citycare/.

Clayton, James. "Bob Lee Killing Highlights San Francisco Crime Fears." *BBC*, Apr. 7, 2023. https://www.bbc.com/news/world-us-canada-65191474.

Cleveland, Christena. *Disunity in Christ: Uncovering the Hidden Forces that Keep Us Apart.* Downers Grove, IL: InterVarsity, 2013.

"Track Covid-19 in the U.S." *New York Times*, Mar. 26, 2024. https://www.nytimes.com/interactive/2023/us/covid-cases.html.

Cone, James H. *Black Theology and Black Power.* Maryknoll, NY: Orbis, 1997.

———. *A Black Theology of Liberation.* Maryknoll, NY: Orbis, 2010.

———. *The Cross and the Lynching Tree.* Maryknoll, NY: Orbis, 2013.

———. *God of the Oppressed.* Maryknoll, NY: Orbis, 1997.

———. *The Spirituals and the Blues.* Maryknoll, NY: Orbis, 1992.

David, Susan. *Emotional Agility: Get Unstuck, Embrace Change, and Thrive in Work and Life.* New York: Penguin, 2016.

Dobbs-Allsopp, F. W. *Lamentations.* Interpretation: A Bible Commentary for Teaching and Preaching. Louisville: John Knox, 2002.

Drane, John. *The McDonaldization of the Church: Consumer Culture and the Church's Future.* Macon, GA: Smith & Helwys, 2012.

Fiddes, Paul S. *The Creative Suffering of God.* Oxford: Oxford University Press, 2002.

Fitch, David. *Faithful Presence: Seven Disciplines That Shape the Church for Mission.* Downers Grove, IL: InterVarsity, 2017.

Forsythia, Shelby. *Permission to Grieve: Creating Grace, Space, and Room to Breathe in the Aftermath of Loss.* Chicago: Shelby Forsythia, 2019.

Frost, Michael. *Keep Christianity Weird: Embracing the Discipline of Being Different.* Colorado Springs, CO: NavPress, 2016.

Graham, Ruth. "Hillsong, Once a Leader of Christian Cool, Loses Footing in America." *The New York Times*, Apr. 6, 2022. https://www.nytimes.com/2022/03/29/us/hillsong-church-scandals.html.

Bibliography

Gehrz, Christopher, and Mark Pattie. *The Pietist Option: Hope for the Renewal of Christianity*. Downers Grove, IL: InterVarsity, 2017.

Gilliard, Dominique Dubois. *Subversive Witness: Scripture's Call to Leverage Privilege*. Grand Rapids: Zondervan Reflective, 2021.

Gorman, Michael J. *Becoming the Gospel: Paul, Participation, and Mission*. Grand Rapids: Eerdmans, 2015.

Green, Joel B. *Body, Soul, and Human Life: The Nature of Humanity in the Bible*. Grand Rapids: Baker Academic, 2008.

Gushee, David P., and Reggie L. Williams. *Justice and the Way of Jesus: Christian Ethics and the Incarnational Discipleship of Glen Stassen*. New York: Orbis, 2020.

Hagstrom, Anders. "CEO Blasts San Francisco as a City of Chaos, Closes Store Over Rampant Crime; 'Our Team Is Terrified.'" Fox Business, Oct. 19, 2022. https://www.foxbusiness.com/small-business/ceo-blasts-san-francisco-city-chaos-closes-store-rampant-crime-our-team-terrified.

Hall, Douglas J. "Despair in Pervasive Ailment." In *Hope of the World: Mission in a Global Context; Papers from the Campbell Seminar*, edited by Walter Brueggemann, 83–93. Louisville: Westminster John Knox, 2001.

Harasta, Eva and Brian Brock, eds. *Evoking Lament: A Theological Discussion*. New York: T&T Clark International, 2009.

Harper, G. Gregory, and Kit Barker, eds. *Finding Lost Words: The Church's Right to Lament*. Eugene, OR: Wipf & Stock, 2017.

Heschel, Abraham. *The Prophets*. Peabody, MA: Hendrickson, 1962.

———. *The Sabbath*. New York: Farrar, Straus, and Giroux, 1951.

Hirsch, Alan, and Tim Catchim. *The Permanent Revolution: Apostolic Imagination and Practice for the 21st Century Church*. San Francisco, CA: Jossey-Bass, 2012.

Hodges, Samuel J., and Kathy Leonard. *Grieving with Hope: Finding Comfort as You Journey Through Loss*. Grand Rapids: Baker, 2011.

Houston, Ben. "Announcement: Hillsong San Francisco." *Hillsong San Francisco* (blog), Feb. 27, 2016. https://hillsong.com/collected/blog/2016/02/hillsong-san-francisco/#.Ys8hjJPMIUp.

Houston, Brian. *Live Love Lead: The Best Is Yet to Come!* New York: FaithWords, 2015.

Hybels, Bill. *Axiom: Powerful Leadership Proverbs*. Grand Rapids: Zondervan, 2008.

Jacobi, Christopher Justin, et al. "Associations of Changes in Religiosity with Flourishing During the COVID-19 Pandemic: A Study of Faith Communities in the United States." *Frontiers in Psychology* 13 (Apr. 4, 2022). https://www.frontiersin.org/articles/10.3389/fpsyg.2022.805785/full

James, Christopher B. *Church Planting in Post-Christian Soil: Theology and Practice*. New York: Oxford University Press, 2017.

Jennings, Willie J. *The Christian Imagination: Theology and the Origins of Race*. New Haven, CT: Yale University Press, 2010.

Jones, Caroline, dir. *Australian Story*. Season 10, episode 26, "Life of Brian." Aired Aug. 1, 2005, on ABC. http://www.abc.net.au/programsales/s1482723.htm.

Nortey, Justin. "More Houses of Worship Are Returning to Normal Operations, but In-Person Attendance Is Unchanged since Fall." Pew Research Center, Mar. 22, 2022. https://www.pewresearch.org/short-reads/2022/03/22/more-houses-of-worship-are-returning-to-normal-operations-but-in-person-attendance-is-unchanged-since-fall/.

Bibliography

Kamiya, Gary. "SF's Unofficial Port Laureate Thrived in 'Cool, Grey City of Love'— For a Time." *San Francisco Chronicle*, Oct. 17, 2020. https://www.sfchronicle.com/chronicle_vault/article/San-Francisco-s-unofficial-poet-laureate-15651650.php#photo-20115609.

Katongole, Emmanuel. *Born from Lament: The Theology and Politics of Hope in Africa.* Grand Rapids: Eerdmans, 2017.

Katongole, Emmanuel, and Chris Rice. *Reconciling All Things: A Christian Vision for Justice, Peace, and Healing.* Downers Grove, IL: InterVarsity, 2008.

Keller, Timothy. *Generous Justice: How God's Grace Makes Us Just.* New York: Viking, 2010.

Kim, Allen. "What Is a Megachurch?" *CNN*, Apr. 27, 2019. https://www.cnn.com/2019/04/27/us/what-is-a-megachurch-explainer/.

Kim, Grace Ji-Sun, and Graham Hill. *Healing Our Broken Humanity: Practices for Revitalizing the Church and Renewing the World.* Downers Grove, IL: InterVarsity, 2018.

Kinnaman, David. "A Year Out: How COVID-19 Has Impacted Practicing Christians." Barna, Mar. 18, 2021. https://www.barna.com/research/a-year-out/.

King, Martin Luther, Jr. *Letter from Birmingham Jail: The Autobiography of Martin Luther King Jr.* Edited by C. Carson. New York: Grand Central, 1998.

————. "The Other America Speech Transcript—Martin Luther King Jr." Rev, Apr. 14, 1967, https://www.rev.com/blog/transcripts/the-other-america-speech-transcript-martin-luther-king-jr.

Kreider, Alan. *The Patient Ferment of the Early Church: The Improbable Rise of Christianity in the Roman Empire.* Grand Rapids: Baker 2016.

"Learn about Fellowship Church." Fellowship Church, n.d. https://www.fellowshipchurch.com/about-us.

Leech, Tara Beth. *Radiant Church: Restoring the Credibility of our Witness.* Downers Grove, IL: InterVarsity, 2021.

Lee, Nancy C., and Carleen Mandolfo, eds. *Lamentations in Contemporary Cultural Contexts.* Atlanta: Society of Biblical Literature, 2008.

Lee, Sang Hyun. *From a Liminal Place: An Asian American Theology.* Minneapolis: Fortress, 2010.

Lewis, C. S. *A Grief Observed.* San Francisco: HarperCollins, 1996.

Lohfink, Gerhard. *Jesus and Community: The Social Dimension of Christian Faith.* New York: Fortress, 1984.

Martell-Otero, Loida I., et al. *Latina Evangélicas: A Theology Survey from the Margins.* Eugene, OR: Cascade Books, 2013.

McBride, Ben. *Troubling the Water: The Urgent Work of Radical Belonging.* Minneapolis: Broadleaf, 2023.

McCoy, Berly. "How Your Brain Copes With Grief and Why It Takes Time to Heal." NPR, Dec. 20, 2021. https://www.npr.org/sections/health-shots/2021/12/20/1056741090/grief-loss-holiday-brain-healing.

McGinnis, Kelsey Kramer. "Should We Keep Singing Hillsong?" *Christianity Today*, May 2, 2022. https://www.christianitytoday.com/ct/2022/may-web-only/hillsong-church-music-sing-worship-scandal-documentary.html.

McKinney, Kelsey. "How Hillsong Church Conquered the Music Industry in God's Name." Fader, May 2, 2022. https://www.thefader.com/2018/10/11/hillsong-church-worship-songs-music-industry.

Bibliography

McKnight, Scot. *A Fellowship of Differents: Showing the World God's Design for Life Together*. Grand Rapids: Zondervan, 2015.

Newbigin, Lesslie. *The Gospel in Pluralist Society*. Grand Rapids: Eerdmans, 1989.

O'Connor, Kathleen M. *Lamentations and the Tears of the World*. Maryknoll, NY: Orbis, 2002.

Newport, Frank. "Religion and the COVID-19 Virus in the U.S." Gallup, Apr. 6, 2020, https://news.gallup.com/opinion/polling-matters/307619/religion-covid-virus.aspx.

Pillay, Jerry. "COVID-19 Shows the Need to Make Church More Flexible." *Transformation* 37.4 (2020) 266–75. https://journals.sagepub.com/doi/pdf/10.1177/0265378820963156.

Pilling, Janos, et al. "Alcohol Use in the First Three Years of Bereavement: A National Representative Survey." Substance Abuse Treatment, Prevention, and Policy 7.3 (2012). https://www.ncbi.nlm.nih.gov/pmc/articles/PMC3286419/.

Rah, Soong-Chah. *Many Colors: Cultural Intelligence for the Changing Church*. Chicago: Moody, 2010.

———. *The Next Evangelicalism: Freeing the Church from Western Cultural Captivity*. Downers Grove, IL: InterVarsity, 2009.

———. *Prophectic Lament: A Call for Justice in Troubled Times*. Downers Grove, IL: InterVarsity, 2015. Kindle ed.

Riches, Tanya, and Tom Wagner. "The Evolution of Hillsong Music: From Australian Pentecostal Congregation to Global Brand." *Australian Journal of Communication* 39 (2012) 17–36.

Ritzer, George. *The McDonaldization of Society*. 8th ed. Thousand Oaks, CA: SAGE, 2012.

Robinson, Natasha Sistrunk. *Voices of Lament: Reflections on Brokenness and Hope in a World Longing for Justice*. Grand Rapids: Revel, 2022.

Rohr, Richard. "The Dualistic Mind." Center for Action and Contemplation, Jan. 29, 2017. https://cac.org/daily-meditations/the-dualistic-mind-2017-01-29/.

Salter-McNeil, Brenda. *Roadmap to Reconciliation 2.0: Moving Communities into Unity, Wholeness, and Justice*. Downers Grove, IL: InterVarsity, 2020.

Salvatierra, Alexia, and Peter Heltzel. *Faith-Rooted Organizing: Mobilizing the Church in Service to the World*. Downers Grove, IL: InterVarsity, 2014.

Sassoon, Mara, and Thurston, Andrew. "Why Are So Many Religious Leaders Facing Stress and Burnout?" *The Brink*, Mar. 17, 2022. https://www.bu.edu/articles/2022/why-are-so-many-religious-leaders-facing-stress-and-burnout/.

Schenck, Jeb, and Jessie Cruickshank. "Evolving Kolb: Experiential Education in the Age of Neuroscience." *Journal of Experiential Education* 38.1 (2015) 73–95.

"See What God Can Do through You." Elevation Church, n.d. https://elevationchurch.org/about/.

Sherwood, Harriet. "White Evangelical Christians Stick by Trump Again." *The Guardian*, Nov. 6, 2020. https://www.theguardian.com/us-news/2020/nov/06/white-evangelical-christians-supported-trump.

Smit, D. J. *Essays in Public Theology: Collected Essays*. Edited by Ernst M. Conradie. Study Guides in Religion and Theology. Stellenbosch: SUN, 2007.

Smith, Efrem. *The Post-Black and Post-White Church: Becoming the Beloved Community in a Multi-Ethnic World*. San Francisco: Jossey-Bass, 2012.

Smith, Efrem, and Phil Jackson. *The Hip Hop Church: Connecting with the Movement Shaping Our Culture*. Downers Grove, IL: InterVarsity, 2005.

Bibliography

Stassen, Glen H. *Just Peacemaking: The New Paradigm for the Ethics of Peace and War.* Cleveland: Pilgrim, 2008.

———. *Just Peacemaking: Tranformative Initiatives for Justice and Peace.* Louisville: Westminster John Knox, 1992.

———. *A Thicker Jesus: Incarnational Discipleship in a Secular Age.* Louisville: Westminster John Knox, 2012. Kindle ed.

Shellenberger, Michael. "San Francisco is Decaying: And Democrats Have Allowed it to Happen." *The Spectator*, Feb. 13, 2022. https://www.spectator.co.uk/article/san-francisco-is-decaying/.

Swanson, David. *Rediscipling the White Church: From Cheap Diversity to True Solidarity.* Downers Grove, IL: InterVarsity, 2020.

Talbot, David. *Season of the Witch: Enchantment, Terror, and Deliverance in the City of Love.* New York: Free Press, 2012.

Taylor, Charles. *Modern Social Imaginaries.* London: Duke University Press, 2004.

———. *A Secular Age.* Cambridge, MA: Harvard University Press, 2007.

Tesfai, Yacob, ed. *The Scandal of a Crucified World: Perspectives on the Cross and Suffering.* Maryknoll, NY: Orbis, 1994.

Thompson, Mary Jones. "Yep. SF's Population Decline was Dramatic." The San Francisco Standard, Mar. 24, 2022. https://sfstandard.com/community/san-francisco-pandemic-population-decline-census/.

Thurman, Howard. *Jesus and the Disinherited.* Boston: Beacon, 1996.

Tizon, Al. *Whole and Reconciled: Gospel, Church, and Mission in a Fractured World.* Grand Rapids: Baker Academic, 2018.

Van der Kolk, Bessel. *The Boyd Keeps the Score: Brain, Mind, and Body in the Healing of Trauma.* New York: Penguin, 2015.

Van Opstal, Sandra Maria. *The Next Worship: Glorifying God in a Diverse World.* Grand Rapids, IL: InterVarsity, 2016.

Volf, Miroslav. *The End of Memory: Remembering Rightly in a Violent World.* Grand Rapids: Eerdmans, 2021.

———. *Exclusion and Embrace: A Theological Exploration of Identity, Otherness, and Reconciliation.* Nashville: Abingdon,1996.

———. *Free of Charge: Giving and Forgiving in a Culture Stripped of Grace.* Grand Rapids: Zondervan, 2006.

Vroegop, Mark. *Dark Clouds, Deep Mercy: Discovering the Grace of Lament.* Wheaton, IL: Crossway, 2019.

———. *Weep with Me: How Lament Opens a Door for Racial Reconciliation.* Wheaton, IL: Crossway, 2020.

Waldinger, Robert, and Marc Shulz. *The Good Life: Lessons from the World's Longest Scientific Study of Happiness.* New York: Simon & Schuster, 2023.

Walker-Barnes, Chanequa. *I Bring the Voices of My People: A Womanist Vision for Racial Reconciliation.* Grand Rapids: Eerdmans, 2019.

Walker, Wilson. "San Francisco Seek More Ideas on Fighting Fentanyl Crisis Following Chaotic Forum." CBS News, May 24, 2023. https://www.cbsnews.com/sanfrancisco/news/san-francisco-fentanyl-crisis-opioids-drugs-city-hall/.

Wallace, Carey. "White American Christianity Needs to be Honest about Its History of White Supremacy." *Time*, Jan. 14, 2021. https://time.com/5929478/christianity-white-supremacy/.

Bibliography

Ward, Angie, ed. *When the Universe Cracks: Living as God's People in Times of Crisis.* Colorado Springs, CO: NavPress, 2021.

Ward-Lev, Nahum. *The Liberating Paths of the Hebrew Prophets: Then and Now.* Maryknoll, NY: Orbis, 2019.

Warnock, Raphael G. *The Divided Mind of the Black Church: Theology, Piety, and Public Witness.* New York: New York University Press, 2014.

Weems, Ann. *Psalms of Lament.* Louisville: Westminster John Knox, 1995.

West, Cornel. *Race Matters.* New York: Vintage, 1994.

Wilson, Jared C. *The Gospel Driven Church: Uniting Church Growth Dreams with the Metrics of Grace.* Grand Rapids: Zondervan, 2019.

Wink, Walter. *Violence and Non-Violence in South Africa: Jesus' Third Way.* Philadelphia, PA: New Society, 1987.

Wintle, Brian, ed. *South Asia Bible Commentary: A One Volume Commentary on the Whole Bible.* Udaipur, India: Open Door, 2019.

Wolterstorff, Nicholas. *Justice: Rights and Wrongs.* Princeton: Princeton University Press, 2008.

Woodward, J. R. *Creating a Missional Culture: Equipping the Church for the Sake of the World.* Downers Grove, IL: InterVarsity, 2012. Kindle ed.

Woolworth, Jill. *The Waterwheel: Practical Wisdom for 64 Common Concerns.* Greenwich, CT: Cardinal Flower, 2018.

Zuidgeest, Piet. *The Absence of God: Exploring the Christian Tradition in a Situation of Mourning.* Leiden, Netherlands: Brill, 2001.

www.ingramcontent.com/pod-product-compliance
Lightning Source LLC
Chambersburg PA
CBHW060341100426
42812CB00003B/1083